In hypnosis Wendy described hearing a low buzzing sound in her bedroom one night that became louder and was soon accompanied by a zapping sensation, as if she were being electrocuted. The buzz transformed into a violent sucking of air and subsequently was replaced by a siren-pitched wail so loud that she thought her head was going to explode.

Nothing appeared disturbed in her room. She lived alone in a rented home in Los Angeles and had no previous interest or belief in UFOs. Suddenly, a crackling slice of light burst from the ceiling and temporarily blinded her. Her body became rigid and she literally floated out of her window enveloped by this blinding light. A large white, luminous saucer-shaped UFO was beaming her up to it with a golden light.

The next thing she could recall in hypnosis was a laboratory occupied by several gray aliens with the classic almond-shaped black eyes. The one closest to her and acting like their leader wore a white robe dotted with brilliant gold buttons down the middle. This being also wore a shining flaxen sash wrapped around his waist, with braided ropes hanging down the front.

The other aliens wore jumpsuit uniforms and appeared to be subservient to this being. All communication was by telepathy. Wendy felt comfortable enough to ask them questions. The leader didn't say much, but what he did inform Wendy of truly shocked her...

—Excerpt from *Time Travelers from Our Future*, Chapter 4

About the author

Dr. Bruce Goldberg holds a B.A. degree in Biology and Chemistry, is a Doctor of Dental Surgery, and has an M.S. degree in Counseling Psychology. He retired from dentistry in 1989, and has concentrated on his hypnotherapy practice in Los Angeles. Dr. Goldberg was trained by the American Society of Clinical Hypnosis in the techniques and clinical applications of hypnosis.

Dr. Goldberg has been interviewed on the Donahue, Oprah, Leeza, Joan Rivers, The Other Side, Regis and Kathie Lee, Tom Snyder, Jerry Springer, Jenny Jones, and Montel Williams shows, by CNN, CBS News, and many others.

Through lectures, television and radio appearances, and newspaper articles, including interviews in *TIME, The Los Angeles Times*, and *The Washington Post,* Dr. Goldberg has conducted more than 33,000 past life regressions and future life progressions since 1974, helping thousands of patients empower themselves through these techniques. His cassette tapes teach people self-hypnosis, and guide them into past and future lives. He gives lectures and seminars on hypnosis, regression and progression therapy, and conscious dying; he is a also a consultant to corporations, attorneys, and local and network media. His first edition of *The Search for Grace* was made into a television movie by CBS. His third book, the award-winning *Soul Healing,* is a classic on alternative medicine and psychic empowerment. Dr. Goldberg's column "Hypnotic Highways" appears in *FATE* magazine.

Dr. Goldberg distributes cassette tapes to teach people self-hypnosis and to guide them into past and future lives. For information on self-hypnosis tapes, speaking engagements, or private sessions, Dr. Goldberg can be contacted directly by writing to:

Bruce Goldberg, D.D.S., M.S.
4300 Natoma Avenue
Woodland Hills, CA 91364
Telephone: (800) KARMA-4-U or (800) 527-6248
Fax: (818) 704-9189
email: karma4u@webtv.net
Web Site: drbrucegoldberg.idsite.com

Please include a self-addressed, stamped envelope with your letter.

Time Travelers
from Our
Future

an explanation
of alien
abductions

DR. BRUCE GOLDBERG

1998
Llewellyn Publications
St. Paul, Minnesota 55164-0383, U.S.A.

FIRST EDITION
First Printing, 1998

Cover design by Tom Grewe
Cover photo from Digital Stock
Time traveler illustrations by Janine Cooper
Editing and interior design by Connie Hill

Library of Congress Cataloging-in-Publication Data
Goldberg, Bruce, 1948–
    Time travelers from our future : an explanation of alien abductions /
Bruce Goldberg. — 1st ed.
        p.   cm. --
    Includes bibliographical references and index.
    ISBN 1–56718–307–7
    1. Alien abduction . I. Title.
BF2050.G65   1998
001.942—dc21   98-7122
                                                                  CIP

Llewellyn Publications
A Division of Llewellyn Worldwide, Ltd.
P.O. Box 64383, Dept. K307–7
St. Paul, Minnesota 55164-0383, U.S.A.

Printed in the United States

Every object—whether galaxy, planet, man, molecule, proton—has its own time…

Contents

Acknowledgments

I would like to eternally thank Carl Llewellyn Weschcke, owner and publisher of Llewellyn Publications; Nancy J. Mostad, acquisitions and development manager for Llewellyn; Connie Hill, my editor; and my patients who were kind enough to share their experiences with the time travelers.

As unusual as it may sound, I also express my gratitude to the time travelers for providing both insight to and a specific mechanism for assisting our spiritual growth. In addition, I would like to thank Jeff Rense of *Sightings* radio for his support and suggestion concerning the timing of the release of this book. Art Bell, host of *Dreamland* and *Coast to Coast with Art Bell,* has been a good friend and has kindly allowed me to spread the word about time travelers by way of his network radio show. Thanks, Art, for your forum and many interesting Sunday evenings on the air. Lastly, I thank the universe for providing the opportunity to each of us to learn how to become a better soul.

Note to the reader

This book is the result of the professional experiences accumulated by the author since 1974, working individually with over 11,000 patients. The material included herein is intended to complement, not replace, the advice of your own physician, psychotherapist, or other health care professional, whom you should always consult about your circumstances in reference to your own physical, psychological, and spiritual well-being.

Introduction

There are few concepts as controversial and puzzling as that of time travel. We may view time objectively as a form of external change and subjectively as a form of thought. Technology has taken this topic of metaphysical speculation and has placed it within the parameters of experimental science.

This investigation of time travel by scientists, especially quantum physicists, has resulted in a loss of the mystical and sacred qualities of time and its investigation leading to what one day will ideally be a complete understanding of this fascinating concept.

Considering the different concepts of time used in mathematics and physics, or in the theories of relativity and quantum mechanics, to say nothing of the differences between biological time, psychological time, social and historical time, we may doubt the objective existence of time altogether.

What is the essence of time? Measurement fails to express the essential nature of time. Measurement does not reveal the total reality of any phenomenon (or any object), nor is it expected to do so. Instead, it particularizes an actual aspect of reality, partial but so integral that it must be included in any attempt to comprehend reality as a whole.

In discussing time travel we will fully explore the concept of simultaneous time and space-time continuum. The special theory of relativity proposed three cardinal facts in relationship to simultaneous time. The first conclusion stated that it is physically impossible to separate space from time. Time is not a fourth dimension of space, but a fourth dimension of the four-dimensional space-time continuum.

Second, it is physically impossible to separate space-time from matter and energy. The third deduction drawn from the special theory of relativity is that the belief in a universal time independent of all the objects and phenomena it permeates must be abandoned. Every object—whether galaxy, planet, man, molecule, proton—has its *own time*, which varies with the speed of the object. We will see how particles that travel faster than the speed of light can be seen to move in reverse time sequences.

Throughout this book the fascinating possibility of time travel will be explored, and theories and evidence presented illustrating that time travel has been an everyday phenomenon, and that men and women from our own future have come back as time travelers (mistakenly identified as extraterrestrial aliens).

I will also show how these time travelers use a form of hyperspace engineering instead of spaceships or time machines. In addition, we will discuss:

- Examples of people who have traveled backward, forward, and sideways through time, and have documented their travels.

- Teleportation cases.

- Hyperspace travel and hyper-universes.

- A paradigm that shows the aliens that UFO abductees encountered are supervised by us in the distant future.

- Consciousness and time.

- Dreamtime.
- Examples of how some angelic encounters are actually experiences with time travelers.
- Examples of how the same individual has been abducted by the very same time travelers in several of his or her past lives.
- The precise mechanism to explain how a time traveler can move through solid objects and observe us while remaining invisible.
- Out-of-body experiences and time travel.
- Modern theories of time travel demonstrating its possibility and that it does not violate the principle of causality.
- A model of a five-dimensional universe containing parallel universes.
- Past life regression, age progression, future life progression, and parallel universes.
- Self-hypnosis exercises that will allow you to travel back or forward in time and custom design your own destiny.
- How to use these time travel principles to attain spiritual growth.
- How time travel through hypnosis to past and future lives demonstrates life after death.

For the first time in the history of civilization, we are capable of traveling through time and applying these experiences to the betterment of ourselves and the universe as a whole. Neither the discovery of fire nor the invention of writing nor the wheel was any more important in its day.

Be prepared for a special type of revolution as you read this book. No, you won't be taken on a mother ship to a distant galaxy to join the Mayans. What will occur is a transformation through hyperspace travel to a life of spiritual growth and unbelievable advanced technology, the likes of which you couldn't even imagine now. Listen to these time travelers and facilitate your spiritual growth. The future is now—be ready to receive it.

— Dr. Bruce Goldberg
Woodland Hills, California

Chapter 1

A mother and her son encounter time travelers

I t was a low humming sound, barely a buzz, like the subtle white noise of an electric appliance. I hardly gave it a thought. But then it got louder. I froze. The book I was reading dropped in my lap. I sat statue still with the eerie feeling that something was not right. Then I felt it. A zapping sensation like being electrocuted. I fell across the bed, terrified, rapid-fire questions blasting through my head.

The buzz turned into a violent sucking of air like being a hand-width from a fast-moving locomotive. The sound rolled into a siren-pitched wail so loud I thought it would pierce my eardrums. An icy blast of wind flew at me as though I were standing on the tarmac at takeoff. My long hair did tornadoes about my face. I felt my cheeks turn polar blue. Looking through squinted eyes I was flabbergasted to see the lamp shade on the side table not so much as flutter. The wind tunnel somehow encompassed me without affecting my surroundings in any way.

A crackling slice of light burst from the ceiling, blinding me momentarily. I heard a gurgle deep in my throat that was supposed to be a scream. My skin tingled, then throbbed with pain—like being cooked. I wanted to tear down the hall but could not move at all. My mind raced, aching for my son's safety in his crib.

Feeling dizzy and suddenly very tired, I closed my eyes and it became very quiet and muffled, like slipping under the foam of a warm bubble bath. The last thing I heard was my own breathing. I must have fallen asleep because when I awoke it was morning. The clock had stopped.

A crimson drop of blood from my nose fell onto the pillow beneath me. Then another. By the time I reached the bathroom, I was holding a small pool of blood in the palm of my hand.

These are descriptions of abductions that happened to a woman named Tina who we will soon discuss in detail, but first a little background about this book.

We have all read accounts of UFO abductions. Most of these experiences qualify psychiatrically as post-traumatic stress disorder. I do not mean to imply that these are not real phenomena. The Bible and ancient religious works of many different cultures all have recorded UFO sightings and encounters for thousands of years. What is not often reported is that some of these alien abductors are ourselves in the future. Another startling fact that you may not be aware of is that these time travelers' purpose is to facilitate our spiritual growth in this life!

Many of my readers assume I do not believe in or have direct experience with UFO abductees. Nothing could be further from the truth. In Chapters 7, 8, 16, and 18 of my first book, *Past Lives—Future Lives* (Ballantine, 1988), I fully described both past and future life encounters my patients had with extraterrestrial beings.

Throughout my professional life I have worked with nearly 100 UFO abductees. Instead of the well-reported trauma as a result of these "missing time" episodes, I noted a more spiritual purpose for these interactions. I have also discovered through hypnotic regressions that these abductors are *human* time travelers from 1,000 to 3,000 years in our future. Additionally, these time travelers have abducted the same individual in several of their past lives for the same purpose of assisting their spiritual unfoldment.

Tina's case is a most remarkable example of this spiritual quest. This southern California woman in her mid-thirties had called my office with the chief complaints of compulsive eating, back pain, headaches, and nosebleeds. Her son Brad also had unexplained nosebleeds. My curiosity was particularly stirred when she mentioned two other facts. Tina had experienced several missing time episodes, and her young son Brad began drawing pictures of aliens that he dreamed about.

Her history was a book in itself. Tina had a long pattern of bad luck and a chronic case of low self-image. Her white-collar, workaholic and alcoholic father molested her all throughout her adolescence. All of her relationships with men were abusive.

When she finally met Kent, a man with confidence and ambition, she married him and truly felt that her life was taking a turn for the best, but Kent psychologically and physically abused Tina throughout their marriage, especially after she gave birth to her son Brad.

The employer Tina worked for sexually harassed her. When she finally walked off the job after he put his hand down her dress, Kent's anger was directed only at Tina for giving up such a high-paying job! Before going out of town on a business trip, Kent arranged to have Tina reinstated with her former employer.

She did finally quit and eventually was successful in suing this exemployer for over $30,000. Kent soon divorced her and pressured Tina to settle for a minimal child support payment. He also had her sign over all the monies she received from her lawsuit against her former boss even though this money was not community property!

Tina's missing time episodes always seemed to coincide with the traumatic and victimization periods of her life. I should state at this juncture that Tina had no previous belief in UFOs or extraterrestrials. She was raised in a very strict Catholic family. Beliefs such as in aliens were shunned.

This case becomes even more interesting when we consider Tina's eight-year-old son Brad. He, like his mother, has experienced nosebleeds of unknown origin ever since he can remember. Tina also has half-inch scars on her right calf and a scoop scar on her left calf. These are classic in abduction cases in which surgery was performed.

Her missing time episodes have been witnessed by her son and her live-in boyfriend. She has had at least two pregnancies "spontaneously" disappear, baffling her physician. The most recent episode occurred in 1994. Tina has always been mysteriously drawn to the Santa Monica mountains in Los Angeles, but has resisted the temptation to go there. She will not wear watches, throughout her life has suffered from the complaints mentioned earlier, and had dozens of missing time episodes.

She has described some of her earlier abductions as follows:

> The first time I actually saw an image of a gray alien being, I felt as though I was very heavily sedated. It's as though I were under anesthesia, but came out of it for a moment and opened my eyes. Although I couldn't move or physically react, viscerally I exploded.
>
> Oftentimes, an abduction occurs while I am already asleep, causing a very frightening waking just minutes before the anesthesia type state sets in.
>
> Under hypnosis, I relived the frightening sensation of a burning liquid being put into my left eye. I also felt a sharp jab in my left forearm with visual images of the gray aliens very close to my face, looking at me.

During the month of April 1994, Tina had a very strange visitation in which a young girl appeared to her in the middle of the night. She understood that this was her daughter. That morning she was visibly upset. For one thing, she didn't want any more children. Tina was content with just one child, her son Brad. Further, she wasn't married. Although she and her boyfriend were very happy together, he did not want any more children either.

Tina told her boyfriend Roger about the visitation, and how much it had disturbed her. He asked her if she was sure that it wasn't just a dream. She was so convinced of the authenticity of the visitation that she made an appointment with her gynecologist.

On May 5, she and Roger went for a consultation to schedule a tubal ligation. She was determined not to endure another pregnancy. The doctor sent her home with several sheets of information, telling her to think about it first, that it was an often irreversible operation and she (the doctor) normally did not like to perform the operation on single women in their thirties. She said a large percentage of those women who had undergone the operation had later come back wanting the procedure reversed. This often could not be done.

Approximately two months passed after the visitation. It was the weekend of June 6, 1994, just days prior to Tina's last update with me. In that summary, she had mentioned a missing time episode during which Roger was disturbed that she had been out of the house at approximately 3:00 A.M. and he didn't know where she was. He was quite upset that she would leave the house that late at night and not tell him.

Tina had explained to Roger that she had felt a strong pull to be alone that night. She did tell him that she would be back to bed soon, but that she wanted to go in the den for a few minutes. All she could think about was a very strong urge to be alone. Tina remembered going into the den and lying down. She looked up at the ceiling and immediately a dizzy, trance-like feeling came over her. She remembered nothing else.

At approximately 5:30 A.M. Tina recalled coming back into the bedroom. Roger was furious and demanded to know where she had been. He said he woke up, looked at the clock which showed approximately 3:00 A.M., and checked to see if she was in the den, but she was not. Although he admitted that it was uncharacteristic of her, he thought that she had left the property and had not told him. Tina replied that she had not left the den, that she had just been resting there for a few minutes. As they continued discussing her disappearance, she recognized the aspects of yet another missing time episode.

About three weeks after this experience, Tina began to feel that she was pregnant. There were no bodily sensations, but more of an emotional kind of feeling. Roger reminded Tina that her period was not even due for another week, that she shouldn't worry unnecessarily, but she could not be dissuaded. Tina was convinced she was pregnant.

Tina's due date for her period came and went. She was now a week late. She took a home pregnancy test and it showed a positive reading. She and Roger were quite upset. Tina now felt an emotional connection of sorts to this daughter that she had seen in the visitation. She felt she knew her. Oddly, she was already referring to her as Anna.

A few weeks went by. Roger and Tina had countless hours of discussion, attempting to work through their options with respect to her pregnancy. On July 5th, Tina went again to her gynecologist for an exam. By this time she was constantly nauseated and quite sick. She was vomiting frequently. A urine test conducted by the doctor confirmed that Tina was indeed pregnant, but during the ultrasound the doctor was concerned that there was no heartbeat present. She sent Tina down the hall to the lab to get a blood test to check her hormone count. She told Tina to come back in a week for another ultrasound.

That evening when they were together, Tina told Roger that they should be careful and again start using birth control. He wondered why she wanted to use it if she was in fact already pregnant. She had suddenly come to sense that she no longer was pregnant, although her body was still very much responding as though it was. She was trying to emotionally prepare Roger for the fact that the fetus had been removed during one of her missing time episodes.

Two days went by and she called the doctor on July 7. Tina told her that she was getting very sick and could hardly get out of bed. The vomiting had intensified and the nosebleeds had returned full force. She was very weak and Roger was concerned that she was looking quite pale. The doctor told Tina that she had received her lab results. The hormone count was quite high, indicating that Tina was pregnant; however, she said that the printout from her ultrasound showed an amniotic sac, but no fetus. She told Tina that she must have miscarried. Strangely, there had been no sign whatsoever of passing any blood or anything else that would indicate a miscarriage.

Since the age of seven, Tina has been abducted over forty times. So far I have been describing an abduction case that is not all that uncommon in the UFO literature, but as I continued with Tina's case, some unusual differences emerged.

Subsequent hypnotic regressions revealed that these aliens brought Tina to some type of underground laboratory installation where humans who spoke perfect English examined her. In addition, she noticed military personnel dressed in American Air Force uniforms. Now we have a government collusion theme to her abductions.

Her descriptions of this laboratory were quite detailed. She related how a small type of driverless transporter flew about this laboratory. This open-cockpit vehicle seemed self-propelled. The area of this laboratory appeared immense in size and the temperature was quite low. She was constantly shivering.

All through this experience Tina kept asking herself, "What were gray aliens and humans doing together in the same military installation?" Several times she was approached by military doctors who informed her that a "brain test" needed to be administered and that she would experience a headache the following day. This became a pattern in several of her abductions.

In order to get to this facility, Tina had to enter a flying saucer that was very small. She described how she was levitated out of her bedroom:

> My legs were straight out in front of me. I was moving through a small opening, feet first. I did not feel the pressure of anyone holding me. I was floating through the air! I was passing through a small portal-like opening not much wider than my body. The head of a gray entity peered up at me from where he was standing below me. He was supervising my descent.

In the beginning she didn't describe seeing her son Brad during these missing time episodes. Then she related this event that happened early one morning:

At approximately 3:00 A.M. I woke up with a start, feeling a heavy thump. Had I just been dropped on my bed? I have had this sensation many times following abductions. I felt very nauseous and as though I had a terrible hangover. I immediately got up to check my son. My heart sank as I saw his pillow red with blood. As he too woke up, I could see dried blood around his nostril from a bloody nose. Approximately one year earlier, he had complained continually that there was something in his nose. In fact, he compulsively twitched his nose for about six months. Doctors' examinations supplied no explanations.

It was at this time that the five-year-old Brad began drawing aliens both at home and in school. He also placed these aliens in spaceships that were reasonably accurate to what Tina recalled they looked like. During most of these abductions she was unconscious and no information could be obtained through hypnosis when that occurred.

Now the sessions changed. Tina described young Brad accompanying her during the entire abduction experience that she could recall. She began making much progress with her psychosomatic issues.

More importantly, a certain spiritual growth resulted from these encounters that I couldn't explain. Tina no longer felt herself, or her son, a victim. She stated:

> There is an interconnectedness to all experience, no matter how much we judge it or dislike it. There is always something to learn from the events of our life. And we still have the ability to choose a more enlightened path and get in step with our true purposes here.

Soon it began to emerge that the human abductors were time travelers from approximately 1,500 years in our future. They were supervising small gray aliens that were from our time and most definitely originated from other planets. These time travelers considered themselves from Earth, almost with the same patriotism you would expect to see at a Fourth of July picnic.

Unfortunately, I could never obtain any specific information on Tina's implants, or those of her son, the location of the government laboratory, or the names of any of the doctors who examined her. She did describe sometimes being examined by the grays, while other times the military doctor performed various tests. Only occasionally did she spot the tall, blonde, blue-eyed time traveler, always dressed in a white robe.

To illustrate the karmic nature of Tina's circumstances, she described her visits with the military doctors as follows:

> Just prior to the medical procedures, I was fully aware that my participation was purely voluntary and had been agreed to by me *in spirit* before my conception in the flesh. I was not a victim of this; I was simply living out the reasons why I had come.

During one of her regressions Tina described a most unusual scene in this military laboratory.

> I searched my surroundings with indescribable interest. Beyond me I could see fifty or more cream-colored, wooly sheep hanging there, suspended by nylon-type cords. They did not appear to be dead, because there was no smell at all. There was no blood and they did not appear to be suffering. They seemed to be asleep. There were cattle hanging there too.
>
> The area through which I was flying seemed to be like that of a huge enclosed football stadium. The dark silence pressed in on me. I was shivering from the cold. [In my office Tina was quite comfortable and not shivering.]

Later on Tina came upon a laboratory table with an unusual display.

> As I passed the display more closely, I could see many pinkish, human-like fetuses, at different stages of development. They were all suspended in clear liquid and encased in oval-like jars. The containers were like simulated wombs.

Not all of these abductions took place on a military installation. Sometimes she would simply be on board a UFO flying around and telepathically communicating with this tall, blonde time traveler, who always supervised the gray aliens. He informed her that they were from our future and conducting various reproductive experiments on her in conjunction with the grays, along with assisting with her spiritual growth.

During one of these visits Tina received another shock. An alien that appeared to be a hybrid came up to Tina and introduced herself as her daughter Anna. Fifteen years prior to that incident Tina went to a clinic to have an abortion. She was told that day that the procedure was no longer necessary as she was not then pregnant! Tina had had a missing time episode exactly two weeks prior to this appointment. Was Anna the result of this abduction?

Tina felt strangely comfortable with this adolescent, and all communication was done telepathically. Brad seemed excited to see his "sister." He couldn't quite comprehend how he and Anna could communicate without talking, but he adjusted to this situation like a trooper. These reproductive experiments were conducted in an attempt to solve massive fertility problems we will have in the future, as well as the current reproductive problems of the grays.

As we shall see, the only real way the future inhabitants of our planet can both better themselves and ensure their survival is to assist our spiritual growth. They are us in the future. The blonde, blue-eyed, pure humans are always superior to the gray aliens and hybrids. Some of these aliens come from our time period, while others are time travelers (apprentices) from our future.

Today Tina has completely resolved her former issues of compulsive eating, back pain, headaches, and nosebleeds. Brad no longer has nosebleeds either. Both Tina and Brad are on a spiritual quest as a result of these encounters with time travelers. They no longer fear them. These experiences have resulted in a deep sense of joy and inner peace for both Tina and Brad.

Tina recently summed up her philosophy toward life as follows:

> My life today is almost unrecognizable from that of just years prior. It's not that my abductions have changed my life per se, but rather that the profundity of the experiences has transformed my very thinking and thus my entire attitude about all the circumstances of my life. Like someone who has had a shocking near-death experience or someone who has been diagnosed with a terminal illness—I too have found that the

abductions have altered my priorities. I notice the beauty in nature and in my family and friendships, where before I was too exhausted from the struggle to even care. This seemingly minor perceptual shift has spearheaded a complete turnaround in my life: I think differently, and so out of that new way of thinking, my life has changed. I consistently make choices around the quality of my life rather than more things or bigger toys, etc. and this has deepened life's meaning for me. I have become a more patient, loving, and accepting parent than I ever thought possible, I regularly feel a deep sense of joy for no outward reason. Maintaining an inner sense of peace and happiness has been a surprising departure from the old feelings of victimization and grief.

It was at this time that Tina resolved her existential dilemma. She felt at peace with her abduction history. Tina described her current attitude toward this phenomenon like this:

Although the abductions continue, I perceive them much differently than I used to. I stopped trying to figure them out—both the experiences *and* the entities themselves are beyond my best logic. They just are. My feelings and opinions about them are up to me. I can feel like a victim or I can choose to feel curious and at awe with something so entirely unknown as the UFO phenomena. And finally—and for me this was a huge step—it's okay if others think I'm a kook or a liar when they hear of my experiences. I've come to know that others' doubts do not determine my sanity nor affect what I know has occurred. The cloud of shame that I used to carry over me has been replaced by an inner knowing of self-acceptance.

Although the puzzle of the UFO experiences continue, I am now more able to exist in peace with the experiences than be crippled by terror and dread of the unknown. There was a time when I simply could not find a way to integrate such preposterous occurrences into my life. Somehow, I feel I've done that now. I am surprised at how quickly I was willing to desert myself. Although I have never had an alcohol or drug problem, I now find it amazing that I could have been so originally unwilling to have confidence in my own sanity.

My own conclusions are quite simply that these time travelers use a form of hyperspace engineering and enter a wormhole to transport themselves back in time through some type of hyper-universe to our century. Mathematical models for this paradigm are well established, and this concept is consistent with current thought among some of the world's greatest minds, such as Stephen Hawking, Kip Thorne, Yakir Aharonov, Edward Witten, and others. We will discuss these models in detail in Chapter 3.

The sellout of Dr. Condon

In the mid-1960s there was a large outcry by Americans to investigate the phenomenon of UFOs. Then-Congressman Gerald Ford ordered hearings that led to the Air Force requesting an independent study by physicist Dr. Edward U. Condon and a team of scientists, funded by the U.S. government via the University of Colorado.

Dr. Condon's 1,000-page report resulted in the official termination of Project Blue Book. What surfaced later was the fact that Dr. Condon fudged his report to satisfy the U.S. government's attempt to hide the truth about UFOs in exchange for clearing the national security problems that he had incurred with the House Un-American Activities Committee during the witch hunts propagated by then-Senators Nixon and McCarthy in the late 1940s and early 1950s.

It is most unfortunate that the United States government has hidden such valuable information from its citizens since January 8, 1969, when report denying the existence of UFOs was published. This ended Project Blue Book and any *official* interest by the government in UFOs. Many organizations and scientists by 1970 expressed the opinion that Condon's conclusions were incorrect and were the result of prejudice, not science.

This conspiracy to hide the truth was reported in *Look*[1] magazine and by Dr. David R. Saunders, a psychology professor at the University

---

1   J. G. Fuller, "Flying Saucer Fiasco," *Look,* May 14, 1968, p. 60.

of Colorado and Dr. Condon's co-principal investigator. Dr. Saunders' book, *UFOs-Yes!*,[2] provides the details of this sham investigation. This is only one example of the U.S. government's policy of misleading the public, carrying on the disinformation begun by the CIA's Psychological Strategy Board in the early 1950s.

An abduction model

Throughout this book I will be presenting cases of people who were abducted by *chrononauts* or time travelers from our future. This model can also be applied to abductions by extraterrestrials in our present time period. I will be using a five-stage model.

Stage 1 — Anticipating anxiety

The abductees fear that something negative is going to happen. There is no apparent source to this anxiety, and it is characterized by an expectation of a familiar yet strange experience. Sometimes these individuals desire to be in a certain place at an appropriate moment.

Examples of Stage 1 include:

- Obsessively looking out a window without knowing why.
- Taking an unusual route to a regular location.
- Being afraid to go to sleep. They may sleep with their clothes on and feel safer with the lights on.
- Inability to eat or remain calm.
- Odd behaviors that are new and begin for no apparent reason.

Stage 2 — A transition in awareness to an altered state of consciousness (ASC)

This person suddenly acts in a calm and acquiescent manner, losing all resistance to an inevitable event.

Examples of Stage 2 are:

- The appearance of aliens, often in the presence of unusual lights.
- Experiencing spontaneous ASC with alien beings present.
- Being enveloped by a mist or fog.
- Having a beam from a UFO envelop them.
- Being transported through a door or window by levitation.
- Floating upward into a hovering craft.

Stage 3 — Interactions with the abductors

This stage is characterized by the removal of sperm or egg samples, the removal of a developing fetus, devices less than 2 millimeters in size being surgically implanted or removed, and bodily material excised, resulting in scars.

It is quite typical for gray or hybrid aliens to remain physically very close to the abductee, almost in their face. Human abductors maintain a greater distance, and almost never do the actual abducting.

Examples of Stage 3 include:

- Procedures to correct implants that were not placed correctly.
- Medical techniques to physically correct health problems.
- Psychic enhancement by electrical or other forms of stimulation to the brain.
- Spiritual growth training by hypnosis or electronic devices.

Stage 4 — Postoperative instructions and reassurances

The abductors now prepare the subjects for their return by explaining the big picture of spiritual enhancement. It is a stage of understanding, empathy, and projection of love. The abductor in charge of this deprogramming often has a special relationship with the abductee. Most commonly amnesia of these events is inducted.

Examples of Stage 4 are:

- A tour of the craft or a panoramic view of the Earth.

- A guided tour of a nursery and the presentation of a hybrid body (the abductee's) or someone else's.

- A holographic screen depicting scenes of their future or past lives.

- Sexual intercourse with humans, hybrids, or aliens.

- An overview of one's karmic purpose and spiritual assessment of the abductee's life now.

- Various healing techniques using energy-balancing approaches.

- Out-of-body experiences (OBEs) with guided trips to other dimensions during which spirit guides assist the abductee in their spiritual growth.

- A meeting with a group of time-traveler advisors who monitor the abductee's progress.

Stage 5 — The return of the abductee to their normal surroundings

This is often, but not always, accompanied by complete amnesia of the abduction encounters. The abductee often awakens from a strange sleep and is aware of lost time, but nothing else. Sometimes they find themselves several miles from where they were abducted. If they are returned to their original location in which others were placed in a state of suspended animation, there never appear to be signs of the abductor's presence. Those that are revived from their suspended animation state report no memories of what took place during their missing-time episode.

Contrary to popular perceptions, the majority of abductees are not medically or psychiatrically disturbed. Usually amnesia is induced in the abductee, which is why it is so hard to obtain details of these experiences. Often abductees experience insomnia and relate waking up in the morning with a sensation of being "slammed" awake.

We can note several physical signs common to abductees. These include:

- Small lumps near one ear or in the area of the forehead.

- Pressure is felt in the ear, accompanied by a ringing or buzzing sound.

- They have experienced frequent nosebleeds since childhood, and often wake up with drops of blood on their pillow.

- Small scoop-shaped (depressed, circular, or elliptical) scars (one-quarter to one-half inch in diameter) and straight thin cuts on the back of the calf and above the knee, pin-prick marks, and beads of pus in the navel are commonly found.

- Chronic headaches, sinusitis, soreness in the genitals, and back problems are observed.

- Some women report becoming pregnant in the absence of sexual activity, with a subsequent disappearance of the fetus with no medical explanation.

Most commonly the abductee is rendered paralyzed prior to being transported to a UFO, or laboratory on a military base. We will see later how these abductions have occurred in several past lives of the individual.

Some more spiritually evolved abductees look upon their experience as one of peace and tranquility. They look at the deeper meaning of their karmic purpose and move beyond fear. If they recognize that these time travelers have been with them before and are interested in encouraging their spiritual unfoldment, it makes this encounter so much more meaningful.

I always encourage my patients to communicate actively with these time travelers and ask questions as to who they are and what their purpose is. If a memory seems particularly difficult or important, I use a "freeze frame" technique to isolate one specific scene from this experience.

In other words, I encourage my abductee patients to ask questions, view this encounter as a positive one, exhibit absolutely no fear, and remain calm at all times. Empowerment is the only way to behave, and it will facilitate their spiritual growth. This is actually a form of psychic empowerment.

During hypnotic regressions my patients often report being physically cold at the time of their abduction, although they are perfectly comfortable in my office. The missing time episodes most commonly last from one to three hours. Other people who are with the abductee, but not taken away, are "switched off" by being placed in a state of suspended animation. These individuals are revived when the abductee is returned.

These abductions begin at about the age of five or six and continue until the age of about forty. The population selected for abduction comes from every social, economic, and educational level of our society. The paradigm that I described is reported frequently among hundreds of thousands of abductees each year.

The alien abductors tend to be about three to five feet tall and work most often in groups of between two and four. If an examination is performed by an alien, this being is usually taller and thinner than the smaller abductor types, and appears to direct the abductors.

When dealing with abductions, there is a classification system that shows progressive degrees of interaction with these advanced beings. Here is a simple example:

Close Encounter (CE) — The appearance of a UFO within 500 feet of the observer on land.

CE 1 — Sighting a UFO in the sky.

CE 2 — A UFO sighting accompanied by certain physical effects, electromagnetic disturbances, and so on.

CE 3 — Sighting a UFO with occupants.

CE 4 — An abduction on board a UFO, or to a laboratory on a military base.

CE 5 — The individual actually requests this encounter, and is subsequently taken on board a UFO.

Both the Old and New Testaments provide ample evidence of time travelers. Consider these citations (all biblical references are from the King James version):

CE — Exodus 13:21, 22; Matthew 2:9; Exodus 13:21, 22; Isaiah 60:8; Acts 22:6.

CE 1 — Genesis 15:17.

CE 2 — Exodus 14:19–29.

CE3 — Exodus 3:1–5 and 33:9; 10, Ezekiel 1:1–28; Matthew 28:2, 3; Mark 9:4, 7, 8; Luke 2:8, 9.

CE4 — II Kings 2:11; Acts 1:9–11; II Corinthians 12:2–4.

We also find unusual physical effects such as:

OBE — II Corinthians 12:2–4.

Paralysis — Daniel 8:15–18 and 10:4–9; Matthew 28:2–4; Revelation 1:12–17.

Levitation — Exodus 14:22, 29; Ezekiel 3:14,16.

Luminescence — Exodus 34:29, 30; Matthew 17:2.

Hybrid births — Genesis 6:2–4.

Anomalous births — Genesis 18:2, 9, 10 and 21:2; Luke 1:7, 11–13, 24, 57 and 1:26–34

Chapter 2

Who are these time travelers?

Many reported cases of alien abductions are only fifty-percent accurate. Yes, they were abducted, but by whom? Even when sightings of unearthly-looking creatures are reported during properly done hypnotic regressions, or by eyewitnesses, there is no guarantee these abductors came from other planets.

Many of them do originate from a different planet and from our time period, but some from our future come back in time to study us, help us, and assist in our spiritual growth. These time travelers, or *chrononauts*, come from between 1,000 to 3,000 years in our future.

Out of the nearly 100 abductees I have worked with over two decades, approximately fifteen of them provided me with enough details of their time travel abductors to write this book detailing their actions.

I have no data on time travelers before the thirty-first century or beyond the fifty-first century on our planet. The explanation for that is an educated guess that we won't master time travel for another 1,000 years, and after 3,000 years we will all probably ascend, so there will be no one left on Earth to travel back in time. Another possibility is that we simply lose interest in time travel after the year A.D. 5000.

The time travelers from about 1,000 years in our future conduct many experiments on us, and have been engaged in this activity for many thousands of years. Most of their experiments have failed. All of our ancient and advanced civilizations were time traveler experiments. We are their most recent project.

The reason I believe that all of their past attempts have failed, and are currently failing with us, is that their ultimate goal is our spiritual growth, to perfect our soul and facilitate subsequent ascension to the higher planes and God. That hasn't happened yet on any mass scale in history.

Since we are today a materialistic, environmentally polluting, selfish, violent, codependent, and cruel society, their experiment is a failure. I am not trying to be a pessimist or a cynic. Actually, I classify myself as a realistic idealist. These are merely my observations about modern society and its dysfunctional behavior patterns.

The chrononauts from 2,000 to 3,000 years in our future make fewer mistakes. They are less well represented, and still in need of spiritual fine tuning. Although much more evolved than us, they are helping us to grow spiritually so their eventual ascension will be faster.

You might assume that these chrononauts travel back in time in flying saucers, but only the ones from about 1,000 to 1,500 years in our future do. The others have mastered teleportation and can "beam" themselves anywhere they want to instantly.

Those of you that like conspiracy theories will be happy to know that each group of time travelers is in communication with our government and exchange scientific data. These chrononauts are responsible for the quantum leaps in our technology throughout this century.

Our history has been manipulated by these time travelers. They leave clues to their presence and actions, as we shall explore in this book. The very idea that our species in the future can travel back in time physically to interact with us seems preposterous to many. However, this paradigm is based on solid mathematical models such as:

- Caltech astrophysicists Kip Thorne, Michael Morris, and Ulvi Yurtsever conclude that this form of time travel will not violate causality. They present their findings in the *Physical Review Letters* of September 26, 1988, in an article titled "Wormholes, Time Machines and the weak energy condition."

- Stephen Hawking, the Cambridge University Professor and author of *A Brief History of Time*, also concurs that it is theoretically possible to travel back in time without violating causality. Dr. Hawking is considered by many to be the greatest mind of the last half of the twentieth century.

- The work at Princeton University of the American theoretical physicist Edward Witten that theorizes a form of hyperspace travel through hyper-universes by these futuristic humans, thus avoiding the need of "time machines" per se.

- The research of the South Carolina theoretical physicist Yakir Aharnov, a former associate of David Bohm.

- Theoretical time machines proposed by Caltech astrophysicist Kip Thorne and physicist Frank J. Tipler.

Each of these concepts will be discussed in detail in the next chapter. (See the bibliography for publishing data for the works mentioned in the previous four paragraphs.)

Returning to the concept of abductees, my clinical experience since 1974 and working with nearly 100 abductees suggests the following paradigm:

- Abductions begin at ages four to seven and persist to around the age of forty.

- Although reproductive experiments are conducted (eggs and sperm samples are taken), the main purpose of these chrononauts is to monitor our spiritual growth.

- These time travelers (chrononauts) function as our "guardian angels" by placing attackers in suspended animation states to allow our escape. They can manipulate our physical laws to assist us in times of need. We will see examples of this in Chapter 5.

- These chrononauts follow us from lifetime to lifetime. They trace our soul back to our previous lives and monitor our spiritual unfoldment. See examples of this in Chapter 4.

- The origin of these chrononauts is Earth from 1,000 to 3,000 years in the future.

- The past 500 years have seen a significant increase in the quantity of their monitoring and abductions.

- Fertility problems are quite common in these futuristic humans.

- Their physical appearance is often (but not always) that of the classic insect alien, with large oval eyes and no hair. In these cases we find one tall, thin chrononaut who functions as the leader, and occasionally telepathically communicates with the abductee. Several smaller beings are present. Their communication is also by telepathy, but they rarely interact with the abductee. The abductee is somehow shut out of their communication. When pure human time travelers are also present, they are always in charge of the aliens.

- The ultimate purpose of these time travelers is to facilitate the perfection of the human soul to allow for ascension and the end of the karmic cycle. As we grow spiritually, so do they. THEY ARE US in the future.

- There are parallel universes in the future with many wars, emotional problems, pollution, etc. that can be averted by assisting us (in that same parallel universe) now in our spiritual progress.

In my first book, *Past Lives—Future Lives* (Ballantine, 1988), I described lives as far forward as the thirty-eighth century, some of which will be quite negative. The fact that these chrononauts abduct us throughout our past and present lives is equivalent to our zoologists tagging lions, dolphins, and other animals for study. The added variable in these cases is time and previous incarnations.

Consider what it would be like for an astronaut from the twentieth century to travel back in time to the tenth century. With his or her knowledge of chemistry, physics, biology, etc., would the citizens of the tenth century not be in complete awe of this individual? Would they not consider this astronaut a god?

To make this analogy more accurate, consider the fact that today our scientific knowledge doubles every ten to twenty years (thanks to the assistance of these chrononauts, regardless of what the government says). Can you even imagine the technological advances we will make in 1,000 to 3,000 years at that rate? Weather control, cloning humans, underwater cities and space colonies are only some of the possibilities.

Chrononauts use some form of hyperspace engineering and enter a wormhole to transport themselves through some type of hyper-universe back in time to our century. Mathematical models for this paradigm are well established, and we will discuss this in detail in the next chapter.

The data from my clinical cases in this book is admittedly hearsay—"hypnotic hearsay." Although the mathematical models surrounding the physics of time travel are well understood and support the concept of time travel, science is based on skepticism and evidence.

Until proven otherwise, I will continue to support the paradigm of the time travelers and their ultimate goal of assisting us in our spiritual growth. I do not dismiss the possibility that many abductions are conducted by aliens from other planets in our current time.

Time travelers' appearance

There are four groups of time travelers. These groups may be described as follows:

The grays

This is the classic "insect" alien with large black eyes. They stand around three to five feet tall with grayish skin, no ear lobes, four fingers and toes, and are the most commonly observed time travelers. Some of these chrononauts appear as "little whites" or "little blues," who seem to come

Gray time traveler

across as a "kinder and gentler" time traveler. Neither type has body hair. Some of these aliens are female.

Other grays of various heights have been observed, some rather tall and slender. These are usually in charge of the smaller aliens and often perform examinations on human abductees. They all wear one-piece uniforms with insignias that often are triangular in shape.

Hybrid time travelers

These are a genetic mixture between human and beings from other planets. Their skin ranges from whitish hues to bronze, and they range from five to six feet in height. Some hybrid chrononauts look quite human from a distance, but resemble aliens upon closer inspection. Many have large faceted eyes and odd-looking foreheads. My patients report seeing female hybrids.

As mentioned in Chapter 1, it is impossible for an abductee to determine if representatives from groups 1 and 2 are contemporary or time travelers, unless they are told this telepathically and recall this

Hybrid time traveler

memory. In some abductions there are only groups 1 and/or 2 represented, further confusing the abductee as to the time period from which these aliens originate.

Pure humans

About twenty-five percent of the time travelers from our future are entirely human in genetic makeup. They look like us in every respect. These chrononauts have interbred with our species throughout time, perhaps explaining some of our genius protégés in various fields.

Pure human traveler

A common trait to these pure human time travelers is their height. They appear to be between six and seven feet tall, compared to the three to five feet of the "insect alien" types and five- to six-foot hybrids. They are blonde, blue-eyed, tanned, clean shaven, and always appear to be dressed in white robes. The many references in almost all ancient books concerning the presence of "Giants" lends support to these reports.

We read about these giants in the mythology of both Eastern and Western cultures. The Eskimos, South Americans, Mexicans, Egyptians, and many other civilizations report giants having some form of interaction with their society. The Old Testament speaks of giants as "sons of God" who breed with the ancients and produce many offspring.

There are reports from my patients of these pure humans working along with aliens and/or hybrids. Whenever this occurred, the pure human time travelers always appear in charge of their activities. None of my patients have described female pure-human time travelers.

Janine Cooper

Reptilian time trtaveler

Reptilian time travelers

These beings have vertical pupils and lizardlike skin. The little data I have about them suggest they are not out for our best interests. As irresponsible as this may seem, these beings are 100 percent extraterrestrial, and have nothing to lose by our lack of spiritual growth.

Reptilian time travelers are infrequently reported by abductees as originating from other less friendly planets in our present century. I do not argue this point, but they also exist in our future and travel back in time. These time travelers are definitely to be avoided, as they appear to be cannibalistic.

All time travelers wear jumpsuits or robes of some sort. Their own species are often dying out, which is why they conduct reproductive experiments on us. According to the chrononauts, all intelligent beings are from the same conscious energy source, and are able to inhabit other dimensions (hyperspace).

We all end up on the same soul plane in between lifetimes, where we review our previous life and select our future incarnation. This soul plane is the dividing dimension between the lower plane of the karmic cycle and the higher planes of pure God energy. We eventually ascend to the higher planes from this soul plane.[1]

These time travelers possess various abilities:

- They can show us our past and future by way of holograms.
- Telepathy is their basic means of communication, although they can speak.

---

1 B. Goldberg, *Peaceful Transition: The Art of Conscious Dying and the Liberation of the Soul* (St. Paul: Llewellyn, 1997).

- A state of suspended animation can be induced instantly on anyone they choose.

- They have mastered hyperspace travel between dimensions, and can move through walls and solid objects.

- By existing in the fifth dimension, they can observe us and remain invisible.

- They can levitate themselves or us at will. Genetic manipulation of our chromosomes is a routine procedure for them. They have greatly speeded up our rate of evolution.

- The less advanced groups make many errors with experiments, but the more advanced ones manipulate time and space with proficiency.

Spiritual growth—the final frontier

Our soul or subconscious mind is electromagnetic radiation, equivalent to that of a radio or television signal. Instead of being housed in a transistor (as in a radio) or cathode ray tube (television) it is contained within the human body. Neurologists describe this subconscious mind as an alpha brain wave or the electroencephalograph.

This subconscious mind is compromised in its energy quality, and a lower level of its presence explains the cause of our dysfunctional behavior, as well as susceptibility to physical, mental, and emotional diseases.[2]

We can effectively raise the quality of our subconscious mind's energy by introducing it to its perfect counterpart, the superconscious mind, or Higher Self. This superconscious mind has been described as the "divine spark within us," since it emanates from the God energy complex.

In 1977, when I discovered and developed progression hypnotherapy, I also came across an empowering method of facilitating a patient's spiritual growth. The technique I developed was simply a way of

---

2 B. Goldberg, *Soul Healing* (St. Paul: Llewellyn, 1996).

introducing the patient's subconscious to its superconscious for the purpose of improving the quality of energy of the former. I called this technique the "superconscious mind tap" or cleansing.

To comprehend how this paradigm works, consider that an individual's problem—depression, for example—manifests itself physically as lack of biochemical energy (ATP, not the alpha brain wave or subconscious mind). Emotional factors do cause this lethargy, and this forms the basis of psychosomatic medicine.

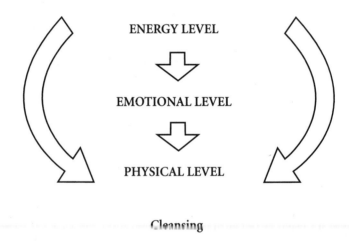

ENERGY LEVEL

EMOTIONAL LEVEL

PHYSICAL LEVEL

Cleansing

However, the true cause of this depressed mood, or emotional component, is not a cognitive thought, but a lowered frequency vibrational rate (FVR) of the subconscious mind. Introducing the subconscious to its superconscious equivalent effectively results in a raising of this FVR. The diagram above depicts this mechanism.

Please note that the arrows always move from the energy (subconscious mind) to the physical, not in reverse. This means that our soul's energy can never be lowered, just raised or maintained at its present level. Our subconscious can directly remove a physical symptom, as in headache pain, as indicated by the arrow that moves directly from the energy to the physical without affecting the emotional level.

By raising our soul's FVR we are effectively custom designing our own destiny, since the quality of all frequencies improve as a direct result of this cleansing. I refer to this as the "new you" technique.

Once our soul raises its FVR, it cannot be lowered, not even by physical death. When we reincarnate we maintain exactly the same energy level of spiritual growth we had at the end of the previous life.[3] The only options for our soul's energy are to stay at its current level (plateau effect) or raise to a higher level.

I am the first to recognize that these time travelers and their technology sound like a science fiction feature film, or an episode of *The X-Files*. In the next chapter we will discuss the physics supporting time travel.

For our current purpose, consider that anything located beyond our three-dimensional universe of length, width, and height is invisible to our eyes. For example, we cannot see time. There are dimensions beyond the fourth known as hyperspace. In addition to life forms being able to traverse time by traveling through hyperspace, they can speed up our spiritual evolution through a complex mechanism of altering our soul's energy by a form of frequency modulation.

Through the modulation of harmonic grids with the energy fields of sound and color, time travelers can use telepathy and both send and receive thoughts from their colleagues or us. They can also initiate a block of these thoughts in our brains, so that we may not receive some of their communication. However, they are aware of all of our thoughts. This explains why many abductees report an inability to "hear" the communication between the time travelers, but they do receive thoughts from the chrononaut that is closest to them.

By means of hyperspace and these lattice grids, our time travelers are able to alter our physical laws and create unexplained phenomena. They explain this concept in terms of *intergalactic lines* (IL).

These IL are responsible for the self-renewal functions of the galaxies. They function through meridians and apparently are based on the same concept we currently see in acupuncture. These resonating IL connect star systems and are open-ended.

---

3   Goldberg, *Peaceful Transition* (1997).

We can apply this principle to our body and alter our genetic coding by tapping into an IL. This is the mechanism used by time travelers in facilitating our evolutionary development to our current species. I refer to this medical use of IL as quantum medicine.

Ascension with the help of time travelers

The main purpose of these time traveler visits to our century is to assist us in our spiritual growth. It is true they suffer from fertility problems (the reason they conduct so many reproductive experiments), but their goal is to speed up our ascension capabilities. As we grow spiritually, so do they. They are us in the future.

The actual mechanism of ascension is unknown to anyone living today. I have always described this as a raising of our soul's energy by accessing our Higher Self and eventually merging with it. Then we become perfect and ascend from the soul plane to the higher planes to join God.

But just exactly how does our soul raise its frequency vibrational rate to become perfect? The time travelers do answer this question, but I must warn you in advance that it is a rather technical discussion.

Ascension is initiated by modulating the level of consciousness, or frequency vibrational rate of our soul, so that it is perfectly balanced. This is accomplished through a conversion orientation of our consciousness to allow it to break through the magnetic fields that keep it trapped on the lower planes.

Now the soul's electromagnetic components are reoriented, allowing it to enter the zone of the higher planes. The soul cannot leave the lower planes and rise above the soul plane unless this reorientation is completed. Our soul connects with the higher planes through a form of geophysical time warp opening. This entire reorganization takes place through many combinations of energy waves.

As our soul is converted into the next higher wavelength, the atomic and molecular structure of the soul plane body is realigned to allow it to finally shed this body. When we ascend to the higher planes, we have merged with our Higher Self to become one with it. Our status in the universe is now one of pure energy. No bodies are present on these higher planes. We are perfect and freed of all limitations to enjoy the true liberation, love, and bliss that the higher planes represent.

Quantum medicine

The more advanced time travelers (2,000 to 3,000 years in our future) have developed very sophisticated medical skills that allow them to regenerate lost limbs and live for several hundred years. Their science of healing and regeneration is a non-surgical approach that I refer to as quantum medicine.

Quantum medicine involves using the fourth- and fifth-dimensional states of matter, and altering magnetic fields with the use of light. The data I am about to present summarize what the time travelers have conveyed to my patients.

Our human body is a microcosmos, or small space-time field, within a larger field. If we can maintain this view, we can recognize that acupuncture is one of the first empirical demonstrations of biological scaling within the universe.

If we are to approach acupuncture from the standpoint of biophysics and also understand the higher force fields that go through the human system as a small, open-ended universe, then we can understand how we can be attached to other thinking organisms within the local universe. Metaphysical literature is filled with references to a linkage with a higher form of consciousness (Universal Mind, etc.). Even psychological literature references Carl Jung's collective unconscious, which is analogous.

In essence, humankind is a floating biological sub-system existing between magnetic fields. The magnetic fields shape the embryological lines of growth and correspond to magnetic grids delineated within the body and the universe as a whole. These embryological lines are controlled by biochemical clocks that, in turn, are controlled by the magnetic resonance factors in the immediate universe.

Without higher evolutionary programming by our Higher Self, we are kept in a form of biochemical slavery within a three-dimensional consciousness by the "apparent realities" of the Earth. In this case, the body is a grid of magnetic fields moving between the primary blueprint of the Higher Self. These magnetic fields are tied together by intergalactic lines (IL).

The IL can exist independently of the Higher Self, but still require the governing functions of the Higher Self. These governing functions are required because the IL grid structures pass through several evolutionary orders, all sharing and working in the same local life space on different dimensions of activity (hyperspace).

These grids are not governed by the laws and mechanisms controlling physical evolution, for they operate by means of their own accretion of energy for maintenance. The body has been left to work on molecular biological levels with only limited magnetic resonance patterns to continue the functions of the amino acids, the basic building blocks of life.

Some time in our distant past the molecular biological levels were cut off from the data transmission system sustaining the mechanisms of higher quantum medicine, as well as the bioelectrical activities of the Higher Self.

In other words, humankind was cut off from the modulating levels of consciousness necessary to maintain a perfected form. In order to reconnect the biological interconnection with the higher energy planes serving higher evolutionary programming, the acupuncture lines of the old program have to be attached to "new" IL (at their intersections) if the cellular grids are to be in harmony with all physical manifestations permitted by the governing hierarchy of the universe (God).

This is the bringing together of molecular biology with quantum medicine within programs of creation. We humans, at this time, are being advanced to a new biological program of creation. This advancement requires our acupuncture lines be extended to IL, which will be connected directly with the Higher Self.

The IL are part of a fifth-dimensional circulatory system combining color and sound that is used to draw from the Higher-Self body the basic energy used for the renewing functions of the human body. Hence, the IL can be used for the complete regeneration of an organ and even to resurrect the dead, when activated by the proper energies.

This mechanism is to be used at the time when the human evolutionary molecular grids are in direct alignment with the higher evolutionary resonance grids, permitting ultrasonic pulsations to allow for direct changes within vascular bodies.

When both the surface structures and internal structures with higher creative energies are attached with the circulatory system (through IL arrangement), a whole new body surface can be programmed out of a skin cell from one or several major sectors of the body.

The connecting points between this circulatory system and the nodal points of cell memory are known as *conversion points*. These points admit sound-light vibrations that change the spin of cell molecules to a faster rate, causing the formation of light micro-fibrils that then allow, in the absence of membranes, the growth of a completely new tissue area or organ.

The light pattern woven by the conversion points controls the pressure points on the cellular surface in such a way that the pressure fluctuations are adjusted during its operations so that the new cells are perfectly balanced with all surrounding tissues.

The conversion points receive their energies via the IL. The IL light exchange, which is stimulated by noise temperature patterns, rotates atomic moments, which are the basic pulsation points in the vibrations of the body, in concert with the normal exchange field. The tissue also receives a renewing stimulus and is able to admit a new limb, organ, or tissue space controlling immune reactions.

In other words, this renewal process is attached with the underlying atomic structure and wave-pulse of corporal activity which is opened to new energies that change the domain walls of growth.

These grids are organized to exchange genetic information throughout the body through a network of messenger cells that are passed on to

any part of the body. The key framework necessary for the proper formation of a new limb or organ is provided through IL grids. This grid
network within the body is connected with the spinal column, which is
the major antenna for the grounding of light signals.

The proper combination of color and sound will establish a healthy
resonance grid within the hydrogen matrix of life, allowing for the
human expression of DNA-RNA to be properly balanced.

Chapter 3

The physics of time travel

We must put quantum physics into its proper perspective. This discipline has taken its share of knocks, and still is ridiculed by both the public and scientists who are not trained in its mathematical models. The classical laws of Newton and Maxwell do not allow for an electron (a tiny subatomic particle that exists within an atom and gives off a negative charge) to be able to leave the atom. This would make it impossible for the electron to emit radiation. Without emitting radiation, a light bulb could not be turned on.

Quantum physics has demonstrated that electrons leave atoms all the time. This explains electricity and many other phenomena. If electrons did not leave the atom, it would be attracted to and be consumed by the much larger, positively charged nucleus. One result of this mechanism would be the shrinking of the atom. All matter is composed of atoms, so everything would shrink, including our planet. The average six-foot-tall individual would now be smaller than a red blood cell!

All of the knowledge of the universe is contained within each of us and within all things

There is an ancient belief that the universe—the macrocosm—contains innumerable microcosms, each recapitulating the features and order of the large whole. Thus man was seen as a microcosm of the Earth, his veins and arteries corresponding to streams and rivers, and so on. In the last chapter I described how our acupuncture meridians represent the geophysic IL of the universe. Let us consider an electron to demonstrate how this is quantum fact. Physicists Richard Feynmann and John Wheeler propagated the concept that all particles in the universe could be reduced to one single particle.

Using the electron and its ability to travel back in time creates a situation in which it appears in two or more places at the same time. By multiplying this effect, a single electron could appear in many different places at the same time, and over billions of years comprise the entire universe.

Consider yourself entering a room in which there are several other people. Now suppose that you walk to another exit in this room, but you have traveled back in time to the exact moment you first entered this room. Another individual watching this scene would see two of you simultaneously, one of you entering and the other leaving this room. You would be in two places at the same time!

Quantum evidence of time travel

A Nobel prize was awarded to the physicist Richard Feynmann for his study of the interactions of photons and electrons. This field was termed *quantum electrodynamics.*

Feynmann also developed a theory of cyclical time involving subatomic particles. He observed that when studying an electron (a negatively charged particle that spins counterclockwise and weighs approximately a billionth of a gram) using an electron microscope, an unusual occurrence was noted.

I should point out at this time that the electron is destroyed when employing the electron microscope. A positron (a positively charged particle that rotates in a clockwise direction and also weighs a billionth of a gram) was destroyed in another part of the laboratory at the exact moment the electron was destroyed.

This is unusual for two reasons. For one thing the positron was not placed under the electron microscope, and so should not have been harmed. Secondly, the positron is identical to the electron, except for the fact that it spins in the opposite direction and subsequently has the opposite charge of an electron.

Subatomic particles are like snowflakes, no two are alike. It was impossible for the positron to exist as such, yet it does exist. Feynmann's famous explanation for this phenomenon is that the positron is simply an electron moving backward in time.

Another way of looking at this conclusion is to consider the electron a positron moving forward in time. In any event, the destruction of one results in the simultaneous destruction of the other.

You may recall this principle exhibited in the hit movie *Back to the Future*. During this film, Michael J. Fox travels back in time by thirty years and almost prevents his parents from getting together at a high school dance. As they maintain their distance, Michael's hand begins to disappear. It is only when they finally fall in love and follow their destiny that Michael's hand reappears and his existence as their future son is assured.

The physicist John Wheeler uses the term "delayed-choice" measurements[1] to describe how our choices now determine what occurred in our past. This paradigm explains how we could have created the big bang fifteen billion years after it actually took place. When we combine this theory with Stephen Hawking's statement that quantum mechanics

1   J. A. Wheeler in *The Mathematical Foundations of Quantum Mechanics*, edited by A. R. Marlow (New York: Academic Press, 1978).

always existed, a strong scientific basis for progression therapy (traveling into the future) is established.

When considering the potential problem of time travel violating causality, Wheeler's delayed choice measurements present us with a principle of self-consistency. As long as there is a self-consistency to the sequence of quantum waves involving the present and future or past and present, our present choices can affect the past and future, and the decisions we make in the future can alter our present.

All that is required is a logically consistent pattern to these quantum waves. Without this self-consistency, one quantum wave would cancel out the other. Going back in time and preventing your grandparents from meeting would be inconsistent with the fact that you are here now, for example. This introduces the possibility that the universe may not be causal after all.

Another law of quantum mechanics that is important to our discussion is the Heisenberg Uncertainty Principle. This states that we cannot know both the position and the momentum of a particle at the same time. When we receive information from the future, this suggests a world that is determined. Don't we now know both the position and paths of our brain particles in violation of the uncertainty principle?

Three South Carolina physicists, David Albert, Yakir Aharonov, and Susan D'Amato, demonstrated that it is possible to determine both the position and the momentum of a particle of the same time without violating the uncertainty principle, or any other law of quantum mechanics.

These scientists showed that if a measurement is made of the position of a particle in the past, and another measurement of its momentum is taken in the future, then both the position and momentum are knowable with certainty in the present. Since we haven't made these measurements in the present, no law is violated. The momentum is still not known in the present.[2]

---

2   Y. Aharonov, D. Albert and S. D'Amato, "Multiple-Time Properties of Quantum Mechanical Systems," *Physical Review* (1985): p. 32.

This principle only works for a process going one way in time—either from the future to the past or from the past to the future. The uncertainty principle is not violated. In addition, we still have free will and choice, since we still must make choices based on the data we receive from both the past and future. Each choice we make determines which parallel universe we follow. The simplest solution is to program yourself to your ideal frequency and stay on this path.

Information is simultaneously flowing from the past to the future and from the future to the past. None of this information or choices (parallel universes) exist until we observe them. These quantum waves carry information to an infinite number of parallel universes that appear to fit into five broad paths or frequencies. We are quite capable of communicating with both our past and future (regression and progression hypnotic techniques, for example).

Parallel universes

Fred Alan Wolf most certainly agrees with the concept of parallel universes, and their ability to function as a mechanism of our future communicating with us now. This theoretical physicist states in his book *Parallel Universes:*

> The fact that the future may play a role in the present is a new prediction of the mathematical laws of quantum physics. If interpreted literally, the mathematical formulas indicate not only how the future enters our present but also how our minds may be able to "sense" the presence of parallel universes.[3]
>
> Our minds are thus tuned or are tunable to multiple dimensions, multiple realities. The freely associating mind is able to pass across time barriers, sensing the future and reappraising the past. Our minds are time machines, able to sense the flow of possibility waves from both the past and the future. In my view there cannot be anything like existence without this higher form of quantum reality.

3   F. A. Wolf, *Parallel Universes* (New York: Simon and Schuster, 1988), p. 23.

I believe that this insight into the workings of quantum physics, a view that I have taken based on the work of several other physicists, including John Cramer, John A. Wheeler, Sir Fred Hoyle, David Z. Albert, Yakir Aharonov, Susan D'Amato, Jack Sarfatti, and many others, is the most important insight into this strange landscape that has occurred since the discovery of quantum physics in the first place.[4]

To grasp the meaning of parallel universes, we must go back to its beginnings. Hugh Everett III, a graduate student at Princeton University studying under the renowned physicist John Wheeler, demonstrated that two alternatives must somehow exist simultaneously if they could interfere with each other now. They exist in parallel universes.

To illustrate just two of these parallel universes, let us consider a classic double-slit experiment. A stream of electrons is projected toward a screen through a barrier containing a pair of parallel slits. Only one particle registers on the screen at a time, while we can independently open or close each of these two slits.

If we close one of the slits, more particles reach the screen than would occur if both slits remained open. Since each particle has a choice of which slit to move through, we would expect twice as many electrons to reach the screen when both slits were open. Yet, closing one of the slits and eliminating this choice results in more electrons reaching the screen.

Quantum physics explains this result by stating that each electron functions as a wave (not a particle) and passes through each slit as a separate wave. In other experiments these electrons did function like particles, resulting in the term "wave-particle duality" to describe subatomic particles.

In our present double-slit experiment, each electron existed as a particle (wave) in parallel universes. Only one particle is ever found in any one world, since matter (our world) and anti-matter (parallel universe) annihilate each other upon contact.

---

4   Ibid., p. 310.

The electron passed through one slit in one universe, and through the other slit in a parallel universe. When this particle reached the screen, the two universes merged. It was self-consistency that caused this merging of previously split universes. Anytime anything interacted with anything else in the universe, this splitting and merging took place. The wave behavior resulted from each split, while the merger produced particles.

This wave-like behavior represents realities—an infinite number of real parallel worlds. It is our observation of this event that determines whether or not the electron reaches the screen. Whenever an observation occurs, the specific physical structure of a particle or event undergoes a sudden change in its physical properties. Nothing is truly real until we observe it.

The paradox of Schrödinger's cat will illustrate this principle. If a box contains both a cat and a cyanide gas cartridge that can be released only if an atom discharges radiation, will the cat be dead or alive after several hours? If no one looks in the box, the cat is both alive and dead in two parallel universes.

Suppose a friend of yours looks in the box and sees that the cat is alive. Your observation is still necessary to make this cat alive in your universe. Even though there is no longer a connection between these two parallel universes (since one observation was made), your observation instantly affects your friend's observation.

Quantum physicists refer to this instant effect created by the observer as the *collapse of the wave function*. This observer in a way becomes a part of this wave. We know that a collapse does take place because a physical value is observed. We, in effect, constantly create our own reality. This is an important concept in demonstrating how we alone are responsible for our spiritual growth.

Our five frequencies

The future consists of an unlimited number of parallel universes or frequencies, first demonstrated at Princeton University in 1957 by graduate student Hugh Everett III while completing his doctorate in quantum mechanics.

Although there theoretically are an unlimited number of these parallel universes, my experience since 1977 in conducting over 6,000 progressions has shown that there are five main categories or paths.

Your five frequencies will be different than mine, since we each have different levels of spiritual growth. One of these frequencies represents an ideal path, and in my hypnotherapy practice in Los Angeles I assist the patient to perceive all five paths and program them to their ideal frequency.

There are duplicate yous and mes in each of these parallel universes. The exact outcomes of these futures are different, depending on our actions and the choices we make. Our consciousness can only recognize one frequency at a time. This is the reason you are not now aware of your other parallel selves in the present.

We can describe these frequencies as follows:

FREQUENCY	SUMMARY
1	An average or slightly below average path and the one you are currently on.
2	A very negative frequency. The worst path of the five.
3	A slightly better than average path.
4	The ideal path.
5	A very good path, but not as fulfilling as number 4.

I use this description to present a typical five-frequency paradigm. The numbers are arbitrary, and I chose 4 for the ideal path simply because it is my favorite number. Your ideal path may be number 2. In addition, some patients have reported two or more very negative paths. Individual variations do exist, but there is always an ideal frequency. Your ideal frequency in your current life is also your best path in a future incarnation.

To illustrate how extremely these frequencies may differ from one another, I conducted an experiment from 1977 to 1981. I discovered and detailed the technique of progression in 1977. My goal was to progress several hundred patients forward in time to the year 2000 to see if biblical cataclysmic predictions and others had any credibility.

The results of this survey showed that eighty percent of these 400 or so patients described a nuclear war beginning in May 1988 between the United States and the then Soviet Union. We all know that didn't happen on our current frequency, but statistically this corroboration of an exact month and year from people who did not know each other is most significant.

The odds against 400 or more people independently reporting the same month and year for this nuclear attack is astronomically high. Quantum physics would state that the mere thought of that event created a parallel universe in which it did occur. So close, yet so far. That is how many of these frequencies can differ from one another. If you expect Armageddon, you will experience it. Keep your thoughts positive and join me in a blissful twenty-first century.

The five-dimensional universe

When we think of the space our body occupies, we concern ourselves with the length, width, and depth (height) of our physical structure. This constitutes our three-dimensional world. Time is added as the fourth dimension to this paradigm. In reality time is the fourth dimension of the space-time continuum.

The space-time continuum describes a simultaneity of all events in our life. To our concept of existence we must now add a fifth dimension of parallel lives occurring on parallel universes.

This fifth dimension is infinite, as quantum physics states that whenever we think of another possibility, we create another parallel universe. My clinical experience since 1977 of conducting over 6,000 hypnotic age progressions and future life progressions, along with over 27,000 past life and parallel life explorations, reveals that there are five broad categories or frequencies. Each parallel universe class has an infinite number of subdivisions.

To comprehend this concept, consider all five of our parallel selves in the same "location" at the same "time." This is a type of hologram. Each parallel universe is simply a characteristic, or optional path of our five-dimensional being. We can think of a past or future event in our current parallel universe of frequency (the one that we are aware of at this moment) as part of history (existing in simultaneous time) and a component of probable parallel universes (never ending, as we continually create additional universes).

This supernatural or beyond physicality aspect of a five-dimensional paradigm cannot appear to us within our three-dimensional world unless we enter into an altered state of consciousness (as in hypnosis, OBEs, or meditation) and globally assess these dimensions.

Another example of this simultaneity of time is that each parallel universe is part of an expanding universe (an expansion that is not occurring in physical space), so it doesn't take up time, per se. Every event takes place at the same moment in time. There is no beginning or end to these occurrences, as we have been programmed to believe.

We can think of physical space as a representation of mental or inner space of consciousness. This mental space contains an infinite number of probable events. Some of these possibilities are contrary to our beliefs and are less likely to occur in our present awareness parallel universe. It would require a collapse of the wave function.

To understand the concept of wave function we need to go back in time to the Copenhagen interpretation of quantum mechanics. The fifth Solvay Congress in October of 1927 proved to be critical to the destiny of quantum mechanics.

The double-slit classic experiment I described earlier was discussed at this meeting. The probability of this electron particle occurring at any point on this screen depends on the intensity of the wave of this very particle. All matter behaves in two complementary and contradictory ways, as I described earlier. In one level, it appears as a particle and well localized in space. At other times, it is perceived as wavelike and not well localized in space.

When this experiment was conducted with two slits on the screen through which the particle passed, an interesting observation was made. Since each of these two slits can be opened and closed by the physicist, one would assume that twice as many particles would be registered on the sensitized screen when both slits were open, as compared to a trial when only one was open. However, the observation made was that more particles got through to the sensitized screen when only one slit was open.

There were two possible conclusions from these results. One possibility suggested was that the wave represented a collection of particles, all of which were distributed through space. This is merely a probability distribution responsive to unidentified mechanical controlling factors referred to as hidden variables.

The second viewpoint states that the particle is a wave moving toward the screen, potentially present at every point on the screen with just about an equal probability of appearing anywhere on this sensitized screen. When it becomes localized it suddenly pops up at a single isolated point on this screen, without requiring hidden factors.

In the first explanation, propagated by Einstein, a collapse of the wave function was necessary. The second conclusion, championed by Bohr, stated that there is no need to explain the collapse of the wave, since the wave is not the ultimate reality. Neither is the particle itself, or reality, per se, the ultimate reality. What exists is one unbroken wholeness that is responsive to our observation. Unless the wave was observed, there was no wave to collapse and no collapse would be noted. This observation was a discontinuous event, not connected to any past happening. There was no reality to any connection with the past.

Bohr's approach provided the groundwork for the Copenhagen interpretation of quantum mechanics. He named his theory the Principle of Complementarity and pointed out that things are only an approximate description of reality. It was a fundamental clash between two opposing constructs (the wave and particle function of matter) that produced the collapse of the wave and the movements of the particle. This resulted in the observation of the *appearance* of reality.

It is our consciousness that creates our reality in the form of these five major paths or parallel universes. Each of these worlds exist at the same time and location. When we choose to observe them (such as in hypnosis), and only when we observe them, do they become part of our reality.

Each and every one of these parallel universes contains yous and mes superimposed upon each other. This applies to past lives, our current lifetime, and future incarnations. Can we alter the past? Quantum physics says we can, depending on the degree of observability. The more observed an event is, the less we can change it.

For example, let us assume that you were a caveman living 50,000 years ago, and you murdered a competitor, Oga-Oga. If nobody observed this occurrence, theoretically it could be altered now. However, we can't do much about World War II; it made all of the papers.

This becomes even more complex if we consider the big bang theory that supposedly explains the creation of our universe. If humans weren't around to observe it, this could not have happened, according to quantum physics. The new physics explains the big bang by stating that we create this theoretical paradigm fifteen billion years later (since all time is simultaneous, it is occurring now) and this mental observation results in an observed event (or possible event) that creates a big bang fifteen billion years ago (actually right now). Now you can understand why, when I mention quantum physics, most people simply walk away.

In the Oga-Oga case we can uncreate this murder, since it wasn't observed by others. This does permit a form of rewriting history, but only to the extent that the event we want to alter was observed. Another solution to this enigma is to simply create a parallel universe where Oga-Oga is alive and well after interacting with you, and switch tracks to this frequency. Now the Lieutenant Columbos of pre-history will leave you alone, and your personal karmic cycle will also bear one less lesson to learn.

Time-loops

When we journey from the present to the future and back to the present we are experiencing a time-loop. This could also be exhibited by traveling from the present to the past and back to the present.

One theoretical paradox with time-loops is what might happen if we travel back in time and accidentally cause the death of our grandfather or grandmother when we were a child. Wouldn't this cause us to be nonexistent?

The answer is yes, but only in one parallel universe. We would exist in the other four frequencies where this disaster did not occur. In the parallel universe where you prematurely ended your grandfather's life, you were not born. However, you were brought to life on the other parallel universes despite this occurrence.

There is no possibility of annihilating every grandfather in each parallel universe, since there are theoretically an infinite number of these other worlds. The fact that you exist to go back in time is made possible by both you and your grandfather resonating quantum wave streams with their greatest strength in a parallel universe in which he survived long enough to allow for your eventual birth.

Each and every thought we have creates a parallel universe reflecting that thought. An awareness is now produced that coexists with our current awareness. We only experience that universe if there is harmony among the layers of these universes. It is our consciousness that registers this harmony. If there is no harmony among these universe layers, no direct experience of this thought-created parallel universe can be had. This demonstrates that there is no death, merely a change of awareness from one parallel universe to another, along with a change of planes or dimensions.[5]

There aren't even atoms present until we actually observe them. In fact, no objects have well-defined boundaries. Consider a table in your living room. Its boundaries would become fuzzy and disappear in about ten billion years, unless we were around to observe it. But subatomic

5   Goldberg, *Peaceful Transition*.

particles can spread out into fuzziness in one-billionth part of one billionth part of a second. The physical universe cannot exist without our thoughts about it.

Our thoughts can actually move faster than the speed of light and as such are known as *tachyons*. Einstein demonstrated that tachyons can be observed in reverse time sequences. The mathematical models for this paradigm are rather well understood and defined. We may state that the quantum wave is a wave of probability moving at speeds faster than light, and it connects our minds to the physical world.

A quantum wave exhibits a double-flow process in which it flows between two events and then turns around in space-time and reverses its course. Our reality is the result of the reinforcement experienced between the quantum wave and its space-time reflected image. This is also the basis of a time-loop.

A sudden inspiration or knowing can be explained by the new physics as a wave pop. This occurs when the quantum wave moves faster than light and this results in a collapse of the wave function, or a "pop." A quantum jump (a movement from one place to another without going in between) takes place both in the universe and in our consciousness at the same time. This results in a sudden burst of knowledge and a universe altered for the better.

Relativity makes itself known to us only when we are concerned with very short times, things moving near the speed of light, or very large distances. Moving clocks go slower than stationary clocks and moving rulers measure slightly shorter distances than their nonmoving counterparts. Here we have an interchangeable linkage between space and time. The discrepancies previously alluded to can be accounted for by changing the appropriate space into time or time into space.

When I regress a patient back into a past life through hypnosis, I repeatedly observe a certain haziness in the information received by the patient. Quantum physics would explain this phenomenon as the past information flashing before the patient's mind whenever quantum waves from the previous life produce interference patterns with this person's current-life quantum waves. Since the current-life electron's wave has a slightly stronger electrical charge than that of the previous incarnation, the past-life electron's wave would be slightly out of sync with the present-life electron's wave.

One simple solution to bettering our future is to eliminate the "baggage" from the past, including past lives. If we continue carrying over these scars and cynical thoughts, the future will duplicate the past. Positively altering our perception of our current awareness will, in effect, change our futures and allow us to improve each and every one of our future and present parallel universes. This is why the time travelers are so interested in fostering our spiritual growth.

Since we now must deal with all possible parallel universes, a different type of space exists. The term *hyperspace* refers to anything beyond the four-dimensional universe, in which time is the fourth dimension of the space-time continuum. We will discuss this concept in greater detail in an upcoming chapter.

In my five-dimensional paradigm of the universe, I included the parallel universes as the fifth dimension. A space that contains all of these alternate realities is what I mean by hyperspace. We can always create another parallel universe, in which objects take on individual, but separate, realities. This is where time travelers pass through on their path to our century.

Hyperspace contains an infinite number of dimensions. It is composed of an infinite number of hyper-universes that can be labeled as parallel universes. These parallel universes fit into five broad categories.

University of North Carolina physicist Bryce De Witt is a major proponent of parallel universes and feels that quantum physics is completely adequate to explain the material world.[6]

What we choose to observe creates what we see and places this parallel universe in hyperspace. Our consciousness gives us the choice. It is also self-consistent to have choice if there is mind (subconscious, superconscious) behind that choice. This mind is electromagnetic radiation

---

6   B. S. De Witt, "Quantum Mechanics and Reality," *Physics Today,* Sept. 1970, pp. 30–35.

(not a physical brain) and exists as fleeting energy in parallel universes. The overlap of these fleeting flashes of energy is the universe we perceive.

Although Everett is credited with discovering parallel universes, I must point out that Einstein's theory of relativity predicted blackholes and parallel universes. Relativity and quantum mechanics took different paths due to Einstein's obstinacy. However, the concept of hyperspace and parallel universes functioned to bring them together.

Einstein, who died in 1955, taught at Princeton University, the very institute where Everett completed his doctorate in quantum mechanics. Perhaps near his death Einstein looked at Everett's work. If he didn't view this parallel universe paradigm in our universe, he probably did in a parallel world!

The true discoverer of the space-time continuum was Herman Minkowski, one of Einstein's professors at the Eidgenossische Technische Hochschule (ETH) in Zurich, Switzerland. Minkowski, more than anyone else at that time, boosted Einstein's reputation and eventual career.

One final point about parallel universes is that we should see as many splittings occurring when we reverse time as when time moves in a forward direction. Berkeley physicist Joseph Gerver's work suggests that parallel universes merge with the same frequency as they split apart (refer back to the double-slit experiment).

Everett's theory allows for this to occur. Now we have a practical explanation of how futuristic time travelers can specifically enter into our world at a precise time, monitor our soul's growth in past lives, and effect changes in our current life.

We may deduce about parallel universes the following:

- Information and time travelers may move from the past to the present or vice versa through hyperspace.

- There are an infinite number of parallel universes that fit into five broad categories.

- Mathematical models exist to support the possibility of time travel, with or without machines.

Anti-matter

I have briefly described anti-matter as the physical substance in parallel universes. We may credit the physicist Paul Adrien Dirac for the mathematical model for anti-matter. Subsequent experiments confirmed the existence of the positron (the first anti-matter demonstrated).

Singularities

There are regions of space-time where large distortions and possible tears in the fabric of space-time appear. These locations are called singularities and they exist in the centers of blackholes.

The laws of physics go haywire here. The blackhole traps everything including light, within it. All physical quantities take on infinite values and there is a connection to other universes in this area through what is called a wormhole.

The Einstein-Rosen bridge was the first name given by its discoverer to this mathematical model. We can see how we can travel to a parallel universe, according to quantum mechanics, when a jump through the singularity in the interior of a rotating blackhole occurs and where the universe layers meet by way of a wormhole, leading to a whitehole.

A wormhole is a connection between whiteholes and blackholes that is constantly materializing and dematerializing. It connects every blackhole with its whitehole counterparts. These wormholes are *time machines* that do not violate causality.

We travel in time to the past, parallel universes, and the future when there is a jump through a singularity in the interior of a rotating blackhole—where all universe layers meet. The very same mechanism that creates blackholes produces whiteholes. One difference between the two is that the time sequence is reversed. At the quantum level there is no such thing as a direction of time, such as past or future. All events occur and exist simultaneously. A quantum foam contains wormholes that function to connect any event with any other event.

Blackholes

Einstein's theory of relativity predicted the distortions of time and space surrounding a planetary object known as a blackhole. In reality, these blackholes are black spheres, possessing what is called the Schwarzschild radius, or gravitational radius that establishes the outline of this phenomenon.

We can look to the work of the physicist Roger Penrose to see exactly what occurs inside a blackhole. These blackholes actually are rotating and trap all light within their configuration.

Space and time reverse as we enter the blackhole singularity. By the time we emerge from the wormhole past the whitehole singularity, space and time reverse again, returning normalcy to our world, but now we have entered a parallel universe!

If we were somehow to reenter our universe after crossing the anti-event horizon of the whitehole singularity, we would observe our world running in reverse time sequences. The inhabitants of this world would find everything to be normal. It is only our perception that would give this world the appearance of a movie running backward.

Hugh Everett III is credited with discovering parallel universes while completing his doctoral dissertation in quantum mechanics at Princeton University in 1957. His academic advisor was Martin Kruskal, who created a coordinate map to more fully describe these parallel universes. In Kruskal's map, he traced light as it made its way in and out of a blackhole in the form of coordinate lines.

This gave new meaning to the concept of a blackhole. The fact that a blackhole led to a whitehole gave it a symmetric structure. While we experienced a past event in our universe, this same circumstance appeared as the future for the inhabitants of the parallel universe. Having now established the existence of both a past and a future singularity, the blackhole functioned like a true time machine, linking two parallel universes and permitting a traveler to move backward or forward in time.

Stephen Hawking, a physics professor at Cambridge University in England, is viewed as one of the most brilliant minds living today. He has worked to link general relativity together with quantum physics. His bestseller *A Brief History of Time*[7] proposed the concept that blackholes actually do exist and provided theoretical means through which astronomers could find them. He also stated that the big bang was one large singularity.

At the beginning of time, according to Hawking, there were parallel universes and quantum mechanics. This means that the universe was following the laws of physics before the first observation took place!

A time machine is represented by this blackhole-whitehole paradigm, in that the parallel universe we enter into may be our own at an earlier or later date in time. This explains the ability of time travelers to move backward or forward in time without the aid of a physical machine. They could enter this singularity inside one of their vehicles (a flying saucer) and come into our world as a UFO!

A wormhole is a linkage between widely separated regions of the universe. Morris, Thorne, and Yurtsever state, "if the laws of physics permit traversible wormholes, then they probably also permit such a wormhole to be transformed into a 'time machine.'"

These scientists further state:

> Wormhole creation accompanied by extremely large space-time curvatures would be governed by the laws of quantum gravity. A seemingly plausible scenario entails quantum foam. One can imagine an advanced civilization pulling a wormhole out of the quantum foam and enlarging it to classical size. This could be analyzed by techniques now being developed for computation of spontaneous wormhole production by quantum tunneling.
>
> This wormhole space-time may serve as a useful test bed for ideas about causality, "free will," and the quantum theory of measurement. As an infamous example, can an advanced being measure Schrödinger's cat to be alive at any event P (thereby "collapsing its wave function" onto a "live" state), then go backward in time via the wormhole and kill the cat (collapse its wave function onto a "dead" state) before it reaches P?[8]

---

7 Stephen Hawking, *A Brief History of Time* (New York: Bantam Books, 1988).

8 M. S. Morris, K. S. Thorne and U. Yurtsever, "Wormholes, Time Machines, and the Weak Energy Condition." *Physical Review Letters*, 61 (13) (1988): pp. 1446–1449.

We may picture the journey a time traveler would experience by entering a blackhole from our universe in the future as follows:

- The blackhole[9] this time traveler would observe appears as a black sphere suspended in space. As he or she approaches the border of this blackhole (the Schwarzchild sphere's surface), the hole enlarges and light, space, and time are trapped and sucked into this aperture.

- Now a light halo surrounds the blackhole with a point of light seen at the center of this sphere. This light originates from a parallel universe.

- This time traveler will witness events occurring in both parallel universes as they cross the Schwarzchild surface. Infinity will be observed. Since all matter will be sucked into a giant blackhole, all of the universe's history will appear, passing before them in an instant.

- As they enter the parallel universe, another light halo is observed and the events the traveler just witnessed are replayed, except now they run backward in time.

To an observer not entering this blackhole, the time traveler's path would appear as if he or she were slowing down, almost to a stop, as they approached the singularity. This traveler would appear to be moving backward in time. Since light cannot escape this blackhole, no outside observation could be made in reality.

The reason this approach into a blackhole would appear to take so much time is due to the *event horizon*. An event horizon is the surface or border of a blackhole. Since it requires an infinite amount of time to reach this event horizon as noted by outside observers, this component of a blackhole connotes confusion. The person actually entering a blackhole would be aware of a finite amount of time in crossing this threshold.

---

9   A blackhole represents the initial stage in the collapse of a star, in which matter is squeezed to produce a singularity.

A time traveler cannot cross the same event horizon twice. The flow of space-time within the blackhole will carry you well into the center of this blackhole. A time reversal results when you cross the event horizon. Time in our universe now becomes space within this blackhole.

Since a blackhole is spinning, it actually has two event horizons, an outer and an inner one. Each of these event horizons are the reverse of the other. Crossing over the outer event horizon makes time and all physical laws appear topsy-turvy. This stabilizes and the world appears normal again once you cross the inner event horizon.

A rotating blackhole allows a time traveler to safely travel from our universe into any other parallel universe by way of any inner boundary. Theoretically, we cannot enter into the parallel universe adjacent to our own unless we exceed the speed of light. Einstein stated that this was impossible. The time travelers from our future apparently solved this problem.

Einstein and time travel

We can sum up the possibility of time travel with a limerick written by A. H. R. Buller:

> There was a young lady girl named Bright,
> Whose speed was far faster than light,
> She traveled one day,
> In a relative way,
> And returned on the previous night.[10]

Einstein's simpler theory of special relativity forbids time travel. This theory concerns itself only with objects moving at constant velocity great distances from any stars. The general relativity theory describes rockets accelerating near blackholes and large stars.

General relativity states that the curvature of space and time is determined by the universe's matter-energy content. Configurations of matter-energy large enough to permit time travel by the bending of time are present in the universe.

---

10   A. Zee, *Fearful Symmetry* (New York: Macmillan, 1986), p. 68.

It requires quantum theory to take over where Einstein's theory on general relativity breaks down. This is where hyperspace theory comes in and incorporates both quantum theory and Einstein's theory of gravity into ten-dimensional space.

Physical time machines

Many physicists have worked out solutions to Einstein's field equations, allowing for time to fold back on itself and permit time travel. Among those are Frank Tipler, whose theoretical time machine will be discussed shortly. The works of Kerr, Kip Thorne, and Tipler are just a few of the examples of these time travel solutions to Einstein's equations.

Thorne's work is truly fascinating. His "transversible wormhole" would allow for a rather comfortable trip back in time. The apparent weight of the time travelers would not exceed their weight on Earth. In addition, the wormhole would not close up during this journey and the journey would require a total of about 200 days or less.[11]

Thorne's time machine has two chambers, each containing two parallel metal plates. The fabric of space-time is torn by the intense electric fields created by these plates. A wormhole is now created in space that links these two chambers. While one chamber is placed in a rocket ship and accelerated to near light velocities, the other chamber remains on Earth. Anyone falling into one end of this wormhole would be instantly transported into the past or future.

The problem with the above scenario rests with creating this wormhole with current technology. We simply can't do this today.

Einstein was the first to conceive of space-time being curved. Gravity could not be accounted for in flat space-time. This invisible force we call gravity is what holds us to the Earth, and the planets in orbit about the Sun.

Gravity can be thought of as a curvature of space. This curvature is in both space and time, not merely in space. We can relate gravity to a time warp—a distortion in the movement of time. This is another component of time travel.

---

11 M. S. Morris and K. S. Thorne, "Wormholes in Space-time and Their Use for Interstellar Travel: A Tool for Teaching General Relativity," *American Journal of Physics* 56 (1988), p. 411.

The physicist Frank J. Tipler stated that it is possible to construct a space-time warping, rapidly rotating cylinder that could function as a time machine. In Tipler's time machine an object would travel to a blackhole and return to its starting point at exactly the same time as it left. This is referred to as a *closed timelike line* (CTL).[12]

This CTL would have to twice move through a rotating blackhole in order to accomplish this. Tipler's time machine varies the path of the time traveler, using an oscillating rather than a continuous movement from past to future. This prevents the time traveler from becoming stretched into a stream of atoms while moving through the blackhole due to the distortion of space and time in the blackhole itself.

When flat space-time was the model, it was impossible to time travel, unless the traveler exceeded the speed of light. This does not apply to curved space-time. Besides, we suspect subatomic particles do move faster than light speed. These particles are called *tachyons*.

Hyperspace

All of our scientific technology simply cannot provide us with experimental evidence for any dimension beyond the fourth dimension. We can see the length, width, and breadth (three dimensions) of an object. Our physics labs have amply demonstrated the space-time continuum, and the curved nature of this component of our universe.

Anything beyond the fourth dimension (the time component of the space-time continuum) simply must remain as mathematical models. These dimensions do indeed exist. My five frequencies parallel universe model is a five-dimensional paradigm. We will shortly see that the theoretical models demonstrate a ten and twenty-six dimensional universe.

Several Nobel laureates subscribe to the hyperspace theory. This paradigm is also referred to as the Kaluza-Klein theory and supergravity. Its most sophisticated model is known as the superstring theory, which specifically predicts ten dimensions.

---

12 F. J. Tipler, "Rotating Cylinders and the Possibility of Global Causality Violation," *Physical Review* D. 9 (1974), p. 2203.

This higher-dimensional space concept brilliantly unifies all known physical phenomena in an amazingly simple framework. The unified theory that results is what eluded Einstein for the last thirty years of his life.

To illustrate how simplicity is a natural part of science, consider mapping the continent of North America. You could travel around its borders thousands of times, taking detailed notes along the way. But what would your map look like? It is not likely to accurately reflect the true outline of this great continent.

Now consider obtaining an aerial view of North America from the vantage point of a flying craft of some sort. Would this not present an accurate outline of North America? Just think of how much time and energy you saved by not having to make all of those trips, and you ended up with a perfectly accurate map.

We cannot lump together the laws of gravity and light, simply because they adhere to very different mathematics and physical assumptions. By using the fifth dimension we can now arrive at a unified theory demonstrating that both light and gravity are merely vibrations in the fifth dimension. This hyperspace theory provides plenty of latitude to explain the forces of our universe in a self-contained and simplistic fashion.

Matter is also viewed as vibrating from the fifth dimension that ripples along through the fabric of space-time. To travel back or forward in time only requires a stretching of the fabric of space-time until it tears, producing a wormhole into another universe and a different era of time.

The Kaluza-Klein theory

It is ironic that the Institute for Advanced Study at Princeton University is the location of one of the most prolific centers on hyperspace research. The irony is that Einstein spent the last decades of his life there, and vehemently opposed such disciplines as quantum mechanics and anything that superseded his relativity theory.

We must give Einstein his true credit. He realized that force is a consequence of geometry, and was able to discover that the curvature of space-time is due to the presence of matter-energy. Einstein precisely laid out the equations to describe the gravitational field.

But Einstein's attempt to discover the "theory of everything," or the unified field theory, explaining all of the forces found in nature, failed. Theodr Kaluza, a mathematician at the University of Konigsberg in Germany, wrote Einstein a letter in 1919 proposing a uniting of Einstein's theory of gravity with Maxwell's light theory by way of the fifth dimension of hyperspace.

Kaluza was proposing a genuine field theory showing that light is an effect created by the rippling of this higher dimension. Writing down Einstein's well-established field equations for gravity in five dimensions, instead of the usual four, provided room for Maxwell's theory of light, and thus brought together the two greatest field theories known to science.

The warping of the geometry of hyperspace created light. Einstein held up the publication of Kaluza's paper for two years before finally submitting it for publication. This concept of using the fifth dimension (previously no practical use was made of it) to write the laws of physics was unprecedented in science.

The location of the fifth dimension is tricky to describe. Since this dimension is topologically identical to a circle, anyone walking in its direction would eventually find themselves back where they began. The five-dimensional universe is topologically equivalent to a cylinder.

Another problem with locating this fifth dimension is that it is too small to measure. It collapsed down to a circle so small that even atoms could not fit inside it. Yet this very same dimension allows us to travel back and forward through time, and contains all of the forces of nature. Now you can understand why this theory is so controversial.

Since physicists couldn't possibly measure this paradigm, it could never be proved. Although it provided for a purely geometric foundation to the forces of nature, as a theory it was dead by the 1930s. The wave of interest in quantum physics dominated the next sixty years until finally this theory was resurrected.

The superstring theory

One of the dominant figures in the world of theoretical physics today is Edward Witten of the Institute for Advanced Study in Princeton University. The superstring theory he developed (it was discovered in 1968 by Veneziano and Sozoki) claims to unite Einstein's theory of gravity with quantum physics. One interesting aspect of this theory is that strings can vibrate self-consistently in ten and twenty-six dimensions. No other number of dimensions works with this mathematical model.

The heart and soul of the superstring theory is that it explains the nature of both space-time and matter. Witten is attempting to find the origin of this theory, and with it the very moment of creation.

Matter in the form of particles is merely the modes of a vibrating string. Because this string is approximately 100 billion billion times smaller than a proton, each mode of vibration represents a distinct particle in the form of a resonance vibrating at a distinct frequency.

The subatomic particles we study in physics labs are not in reality fundamental. They only appear fundamental because our electron microscopes are not powerful enough to show that these particles are nothing more than a small vibrating string. This model of a universe composed of an infinite number of vibrating strings is comparable to a well-organized group of instruments making up a symphony.

This string paradigm explains space-time by showing that as a string moves in space-time, it can break into smaller strings, or combine with other strings to form longer strings. The fact that these quantum movements are finite and calculable, in the form of loop diagrams, represents the first quantum theory of gravity to do so. Einstein's original theory and the Kaluza-Klein theory failed in this regard.

These strings cannot arbitrarily travel in space-time like a point particle, they must obey a large set of self-consistency conditions. Interestingly, when those constraints were initially calculated, Einstein's equations resulted. This ability to derive Einstein's equations from the string theory also demonstrated that his equations were not fundamental.

This string theory linked the quantum physicists' concept of discrete packets of energy that carry the gravitational force to Einstein's paradigm of vibrating space-time. One odd quality of the string theory is that these strings cannot move in three or four dimensions. These self-consistency conditions require the string to move in either ten or twenty-six dimensions.

In 1984 the work of John Schwarz of Caltech and Michael Green of Queen Mary's College in London proved that all self-consistency conditions on the string can be met.

One question that arises from this theory is that of all of nature's designs, why strings? The basic building block for life on our planet is DNA. This molecule is composed of a double spiral helix (a string) and contains all of the genetic coding to ensure life. A string is quite simply one of the most compact ways of storing vast amounts of data in such a manner that this information can be easily replicated. In addition to DNA, our body contains many billions of protein strings in the form of amino-acid building blocks.

Gravity was an impossible component in quantum field theory, but it is automatically included in string theory.[13] Witten states that all the really great ideas in physics are spinoffs of the superstring theory. Even Einstein's theory of general relativity was a spinoff of string theory. The fact that it was discovered before superstring theory was advanced was simply a developmental accident.

This string theory is a relatively simple explanation for the workings of our universe. A string has two types of vibrations, clockwise and counterclockwise. When the string vibrates in a clockwise direction, it occupies a ten-dimensional space. Twenty-six dimensions contain a string vibrating in a counterclockwise manner.

We now can see that the symmetries of the subatomic world are simply remnants of the symmetry of hyperspace. The twenty-six dimensional space of a counterclockwise vibrating string has more than enough room in it to explain all of the symmetries present in both quantum theory and those of Einstein. The laws of physics appear to simplify in higher dimensions of hyperspace. The symmetries we

---

13 P. Dawes and J. Brown, eds., *Superstrings: A Theory of Everything* (Cambridge: Cambridge University Press, 1988), p. 95.

observe in unique designs of snowflakes, flowers in bloom, rainbows, crystal latticeworks of rocks and so on are simply a manifestation of hyperspace physics.

For those of you that may be wondering why there are ten dimensional paradigm surfaces, rather than seven, nine, or twelve, for example, the answer lies within *modular functions.* Deep within the complex mathematics of something called *loop diagrams,* strange modular functions appear in which the number ten predominates.

The mathematician Srinivasa Ramanujan is credited with unraveling the numerical mysteries associated with the string theory. Ramanujan repeatedly came upon the numbers 8 and 24 in describing the actual vibration of a string. The splitting and recombining actions of the string in its complex movements resulted in these numbers appearing in the strangest places. When the total number of vibrations appearing in an equation are noted, physicists add two more dimensions in order for them to be compatible with our world. So the eight becomes ten and the twenty-four emerges as twenty-six space-time dimensions.

It is not that physicists truly understand just why ten and twenty-six dimensions result from these equations as the dimensions of the string, it simply requires these in order to remain self-consistent.

This self-consistency principle is vital to our understanding of the universe. We observe a simplification of the laws of nature when self-consistency is expressed in higher dimensions. Superstring theorists are quick to point out that self-consistency in itself would have forced God to create the universe as he did.

The superstring concept, although not testable by current science, offers us a very interesting choice in relationship to fully understanding our universe and time travel. We could simply sit back and wait for science to muster the energy (trillions of times greater than anything currently available) to demonstrate this phenomenon. Another possibility is to encounter humans from well into our future who have already conquered hyperspace—the chrononauts.

Demonstrating hyperspace

The prevailing opinion of many physicists today is that experimental verification of hyperspace will come in the twenty-first century. To master both the energy and technology to travel through hyperspace is several centuries away.

My hypnotic regressions have revealed that chrononauts originate from between 1,000 to 3,000 years in our future. That factors out to from the thirty-first to the fifty-first centuries! I have no data from these time travelers before the thirty-first or after the fifty-first. This does not mean that there is no life on Earth beyond the year 5,000—I simply have no data from beings beyond that date traveling back in time.

The prediction of the future from reasonable scientific judgments is called *futurology*. It is not an exact science. Since scientific knowledge doubles every ten to twenty years, there are some extrapolations we can make into our distant future, an educated guess at best.

With this in mind, the Russian astronomer Nikolai Kardashev developed a classification of civilizations from a Type 0 to a Type III.[14] We are currently a Type 0 civilization. A Type I category would control the weather, harvest the oceans, prevent earthquakes, and generally control the planet's energy resources.

When the power of the sun itself is harnessed, we have a Type II civilization. This group will also be involved in colonizing local star systems. Time travel will be possible through the use of the sun's energy. A Type III civilization harnesses the power of billions of star systems and literally controls the power of an entire galaxy. They most likely will be able to manipulate space-time at their discretion. Time travel will be routine for these beings.

Interestingly, the prediction for when our Type 0 civilization will reach that of a Type I is only about 150 years. Another 1,000 years is estimated necessary to advance to a Type II civilization. That would put us into the thirty-third century, give or take. My 1,000- to 3,000-year future chrononauts fit nicely into the futurologist's predictions.

---

14 C. Sagon, *Cosmos* (New York: Random House, 1980).

The time it would require to convert a Type II civilization into a Type III is several thousand years, putting us now well beyond the year 6,000 or 7,000. That would explain why the time travelers have so many failed experiments. They are only a Type II civilization, with limited ability to harness energy and manipulate space-time and hyperspace.

Hyperspace and the forces of nature

Thomas Banchoff, chairman of the mathematics department at Brown University, has written computer programs that permit us to project shadows of higher dimensional objects onto flat, two-dimensional computer screens. We cannot visualize the higher dimensions because our evolution has developed to see only three-dimensional objects, such as an animal approaching us. Natural selection did not allow for us to see into the fourth dimension or higher.

Peter Freund was an early pioneers on hyperspace theories. This professor of theoretical physics at the University of Chicago's Enrico Fermi Institute emphasized that the laws of nature become simpler and elegant when they are expressed in higher dimensions, their natural home.

Hyperspace provides us with enough "room" to unify all known physical forces. The four forces of nature we study appear fragmented in our three dimensional laboratories, but when we display these forces in higher-dimensional space-time, they become simple and powerful.

These four natural forces are:

- **Electromagnetic force**—Electricity, light and magnetism comprise this force.

- **The strong nuclear force**—This energy fuels the stars. All life on Earth owes its very existence to the energy from our Sun (a star).

- **The weak nuclear force**—Radioactive decay is an example of this force.

- **Gravitational force**—This force is responsible for keeping all planets in their orbits. All of us and our atmosphere would be flung into space without this force. The world itself would nova (explode) if devoid of gravity.

Hyperspace theory explains that all of nature's forces are different vibrations in hyperspace. All matter and the forces that hold them together in an infinite variety of complex forms can be understood with this paradigm.

The Kaluza-Klein theory was the first hyperspace theory, explaining light as vibrations in the fifth dimension. Next came the supergravity theory, a more advanced form of the Kaluza-Klein theory. Finally, the superstring theory stating that all matter consists of tiny vibrating strings attempts to unify Einstein's and quantum physics' field theories.

A wormhole time machine trip

Throughout our planet there are phenomena in our atmosphere known as electronic vacuum fluctuations. These theoretically prevent time travel by destroying a wormhole when some advanced being attempts to transform this wormhole into a time machine. By becoming infinitely violent, these electronic vacuum fluctuations could very well nullify the use of a wormhole for time travel.

According to Caltech's astrophysicist Kip Thorne, electromagnetic vacuum fluctuations in the universe "are infinitely intense only for a vanishingly short period of time. They rise to their peak at precisely the instant when it is first possible to use the wormhole for backward time travel."

Later on he stated that "vacuum fluctuations cannot prevent the formation of or existence of closed timelike curves (time machines)." Thorne applied the laws of quantum fields in curved space-time to arrive at his calculations and conclusion.[15]

Just what would a trip be like through this wormhole time machine? Let us assume a being from our future (say the thirty-fifth century) established a wormhole in his laboratory. One mouth of this wormhole would be located in the thirty-fifth century, while the other would be in 1999. Internally these mouths experience the same flow of time, but externally they are 1500 years apart!

It is not difficult to imagine our future time traveler entering this wormhole from the thirty-fifth century and emerging in 1999, but where is the wormhole in 1999 and how did it appear out of nowhere? Part of

---

15 K. S. Thorne, *Black Holes & Time Warps: Einstein's Outrageous Legacy* (New York: W. W. Norton & Co., 1994), pp. 518–519.

Thorne's model states that this wormhole is kept open to permit time travel by "exotic material," and we don't have any such matter in 1999.

The answer comes from Thorne again and his calculations. He states, "From a single wormhole, an infinitely advanced civilization can make a time machine."[16] Now we have a theoretical answer to this puzzle. Only one wormhole in the future, when this exotic matter will be developed, is required. Also, instead of electromagnetic vacuum fluctuations piling up on and reinforcing themselves between the two mouths and throughout the wormhole and destroying it, the wormhole defocuses this energy and reduces the pileup so that a weakened beam of energy results and the wormhole is able to bring our time traveler back to 1999.

Does God exist?

The time traveler's main purpose in visiting us is not to abduct twentieth-century humans for genetic studies, but to accelerate our spiritual development so that we (they in the future) can ascend to join God. Just how do physicists view God?

Nobel laureate Eugene Wigner insisted that quantum theory proves the existence of some form of universal cosmic consciousness in the universe. Since all observations imply the existence of an observer and consciousness, for the universe to have been created it would have to have been observed by a greater consciousness, God.

We can look to hyperspace theory for a source of Creation. Before the Big Bang our cosmos was an unstable, ten-dimensional universe. Interdimensional travel was readily available. At some time this unstable, ten-dimensional universe split, creating a four- and six-dimensional pair of universes.

Those two universes reacted in opposite ways. Our four-dimensional universe expanded in an explosive fashion, while our twin six-dimensional universe contracted so violently that it shrank into an infinitesimally small speck. This Big Bang was a cracking of space and time. Did God cause this chain reaction? I believe God did, but you will have to decide that for yourself.

---

16 Ibid. p. 502.

Chapter 4

Abductions in several past lives by the same time travelers

The abductions of Roger

In 1993 I received a call from an East Coast real estate developer named Roger. He didn't appear to have any problems per se. In fact, his life was a rather fulfilling one. Ten years earlier things had been quite different. Roger, then in his early thirties, was a compulsive gambler, smoker, and womanizer. This caused many problems in his personal (he is married) and professional life.

Suddenly his life turned around. He gave up his compulsive habits and developed an overly spiritual but satisfying lifestyle. Roger became even more successful as a real estate developer, and engaged in philanthropic pursuits. He built halfway houses for drug rehabilitation centers, and gave quite a bit of money to various charities.

Fortunately, Roger's wife was very forgiving and stayed with him through his personal crisis. This all seemed great, but I was curious as to why he called me. It seemed that just prior to Roger's turnaround, he had a missing time episode. After reading my first book, *Past Lives—Future Lives,* he decided that I was the one person who could assist him in discovering just what exactly had happened.

Prior to his revelation, Roger had no belief in reincarnation, and lived a rather hedonistic and selfish life. Now things were quite different. He developed an intense interest in metaphysics and reincarnation, and my first book apparently had a significant effect upon him.

The one problem Roger had with my book concerned the chapter titled "Hubert Meets Aliens in Egypt." He felt that Hubert's descriptions of how the pyramids at Giza were constructed was somehow inaccurate. Roger didn't know exactly what was the problem, just that something seemed out of sync.

We will discuss Hubert's case in more detail in Chapter 7. For our current purposes let me simply state that Hubert described alien beings known as the "directors" supervising the pyramid construction, using a type of crane that was powered by a battery and special ropes that were extremely durable. Roger again could not pinpoint precisely what bothered him about this case, just that it made him feel uncomfortable.

Roger's initial age regression to 1983 proved to be very memorable. He was an average-depth hypnotic patient, and recalled an incident that took place in the spring of 1983. Roger was then at a low ebb of his life, gambling and losing too much money, smoking heavily, and his wife had overheard a conversation he had with his latest girlfriend.

Roger liked to do some of the building on his construction site, and he had cut himself one afternoon nearly a month before. His physician treated this cut, but it just wouldn't heal.

The hypnotic age regression placed him in his basement of his home. He was drinking heavily, trying to drown the effects of the most recent fight with his wife over his latest episode of adultery. She had threatened to leave him if he didn't get his act together.

Suddenly, a group of three gray insect aliens, about four feet tall, appeared before him. He had no idea how they entered the room. One approached him and telepathically said, "Don't be afraid." Roger was placed in some sort of suspended animation state and levitated out of the basement window to his backyard.

It was past midnight and although Roger was conscious, he could not move. A beam of light enveloped him and two of his three abductors, and they rose up to an awaiting disc-shaped craft.

The aliens said nothing as they were transported to the ship. One gray stayed behind and, Roger later found out, placed his wife in suspended animation while guarding her.

As they approached the ship Roger, always a detail-oriented individual, carefully observed the craft. It appeared to be about sixty feet in diameter and had the look of aluminum, as it was silver in color. He could not make out any physical seams, rivets, or weld markings on this spaceship. Roger's construction-oriented mind was quite functional during this process.

On board the ship itself, the gray who communicated with him earlier said to him telepathically, "We're here to help you in many ways." He was given a white garment to wear. For some reason Roger could not recall taking off his clothes and putting on this garment.

The next thing he recalled in hypnosis was lying on an examining table made of some type of metal and having a green liquid sponged over his exposed arms, legs, and face. Next Roger experienced a tingling sensation throughout his entire body.

A procedure was initiated to remove some fluid behind his left eye, samples of tissues from his thigh and calf and finally a sperm sample. A metal cup of some sort was placed over his penis, which made his sex organ feel warm and tingly. The next thing he sensed was an orgasmic sensation and he noted a vial collecting a sample of his sperm.

Roger's body felt paralyzed during this entire procedure. He observed two grays and now a hybrid alien assisting these grays during the examination. The gray who communicated with Roger before then moved very close to his face and stared into his eyes.

This was a form of alien hypnosis that produced an indescribable sense of warmth and love in Roger's awareness. It was at this time that this gray informed Roger that this examination was part of his monitoring by them. This was only one in a series of abductions that Roger had experienced throughout his life, but that he was not permitted to remember.

Shortly after this communication, Roger was taken to a room with a small table and comfortable chairs. He sat in one of them, now fully clothed, although he could not recall how he got dressed. A few minutes later a tall human with blonde hair and "piercing blue eyes" entered.

This human, a chrononaut, was wearing a white robe and had a rather rugged look to him, but projected warmth and spirituality nonetheless. He informed Roger that this examination was part of a reproductive experiment, in addition to facilitating Roger's own spiritual growth.

All communication was done telepathically. Then the human, now accompanied by the two grays and hybrid that brought Roger to this ship, informed him that they were time travelers from about 1,500 years in the future. The chrononaut emphasized the fact that certain procedures would be performed to assist Roger in turning his life around, and that he would have no memories of this event "for quite some time."

The grays and hybrid alien were the only other beings Roger noted on board this ship. He couldn't see how it was being monitored or flown. It was explained to him that the ship moved by internally produced gravitation fields that resulted in both physical movement in space and a distortion of the space-time continuum so these time travelers could travel back in time. (Recall my discussion of hyperspace in Chapter 3.) In the center of this ship was located some type of reactor that produced anti-matter. This anti-matter then reacted with matter and created a carefully controlled annihilation reaction that effectively created a tear in space-time.

Then Roger was fitted with some kind of helmet that emitted a green light beam designed to energize him physically and spiritually. A gun of sorts then emitted a similar beam of green light directly on the sore located on his right hand.

The human time traveler reiterated the phrase "don't be afraid," and let Roger know that the aliens were apprentices, but competent at their jobs. Shortly after this procedure, Roger was beamed back down to his backyard, accompanied by the same two gray aliens.

When he returned to the ground the third alien that had remained behind joined the other two and was beamed back to the ship. Roger, in a trance-like state, went up to bed and had no memories of this incident the following morning.

His wife reported nothing unusual except for the fact that the sore on Roger's right hand was completely gone! She asked him if he had it surgically removed. Roger was confused and could not answer her question. The last thing he remembered was drinking the previous evening and staring at his sore, thinking about his unfulfilled life.

Now Roger acted like a new man. He felt and appeared younger. He immediately stopped drinking, gave up smoking, broke up with his girlfriend, and hasn't gambled since that fateful day.

Needless to say, his wife was quite pleased with the turn of events. I asked Roger if this day was the turning point of his life that apparently resulted in his physical, emotional, and spiritual metamorphosis, and he readily affirmed that it was.

Roger's physician had never seen such a stubborn sore disappear so quickly, and without leaving a trace that it ever existed. My inquiries as to other missing time episodes drew a blank. The time travelers clearly stated that they had abducted Roger throughout his life, but Roger could not recall any such missing time episodes.

His thighs and calfs were a little sore following that abduction, but no scars were visible. As Roger was an out-of-town patient, he was scheduled for the rest of the week, and his next appointment was for the following morning. This second appointment proved even more enlightening in reference to his relationship to these mysterious time travelers. His curiosity about a possible past life was stimulated, especially in relationship to ancient Egypt.

Roger's first past life regression brought him back to ancient Egypt, during the time of the construction of the Pyramid of Giza. He described himself as a type of master builder, supervising a large crew of slaves.

When I asked how he managed to move those great stones into their proper place, he described a small craft that he repeatedly referred to as the *anti-gravity flying craft*.

This pyramid-shaped flying car hovered from six to nine feet above the ground. It seemed to blow a constant stream of air down from the center of its underside to maintain its hovering capacity. Roger noted two small circular anti-gravity generators that were used to move and place the large and heavy stones of the pyramid.

There were at least three of these cars present. These vehicles had multidimensional properties and could alter the magnetic lines of force (IL) at the Giza basin and lift the huge stones. Movement of these crafts was by a continual pulse which could alter both the speed and altitude of this vehicle instantly.

There were eight small circular lights on the underside of the craft, and five large ones on the sides of this craft, near the angles of the triangle, but one of these five lights was placed directly in the back of this vehicle. There was a triangular-shaped insignia on the hood of the craft, between the cockpit and the apex of the triangle. The cockpit seated two people. Usually only one gray alien was driving it.

This was a somewhat lonely past life for Roger. He had no family and was very much involved with the culture's religion, the Mystery Schools. As a builder he described being a member of a guild (probably the first Masons), which educated him as to the various secrets of the universe.

One evening after dinner Roger went for a walk. He suddenly saw a blinding white light, and the next thing he knew he was on board a spaceship. This was not just any space craft, but the same one that he was taken to in 1983. In it were the same grays, hybrid, and white-robed time travelers that he described the previous day.

Roger was again informed that he was not to fear any procedures soon to begin. Some of the tests he felt performed were similar to what he described during his 1983 abduction, but this time he was administered an injection of some form of blue fluid and a type of hypnotic suggestion with flashing multicolored lights was given to him telepathically.

I could not obtain much more information about exactly what happened next. My assumption is that Roger became unconscious. Once a person loses consciousness, all memories of events become impossible to retrieve through hypnosis. The next thing Roger recalled was being back in his bed the following morning.

Apparently, Roger was quite good at his job in the life we were exploring. He was given extra rations and a female to keep him company after certain phases of the pyramid construction were completed. His natural curiosity was aroused—who were these abductors? When he asked about them at the worksite he was told to keep his mouth shut and not ask questions.

Although Roger was a skillful builder in ancient Egypt, he did not do well with people. When he attended a meeting of his guild he again broached the topic of his abduction to the elders. They were discussing some principles of philosophy and what we would term metaphysics. (This leads to the conclusion that this group unquestionably were the first, or one of the first, Masons. We will discuss the Masons in greater detail in Chapter 9.)

The elders of this builder's guild warned Roger not to discuss his abduction, and cautioned him about telling others of their secret doctrine (the Mysteries). Any violation of that rule was punishable by death. Roger acknowledged that law and swore he would not divulge what they discussed.

Over the next several weeks Roger was abducted two more times. He had partial memories of these incidents and sought the counsel of some of his fellow workers to try to make sense of it. They were a curious lot and asked him to relate to them what he did during those secret meetings.

Roger felt comfortable with these men. Unwisely he freely discussed the Mysteries he learned, and what he could recall of the abductions. Two nights later one of the guild members slipped into his tent and stabbed Roger to death for violating his oath of secrecy.

After this regression session ended, Roger had several questions about ancient Egypt, the Masons, and anti-gravity flying crafts. His version definitely conflicted with the battery-run cranes and ropes described by Hubert.

Roger's time travelers looked nothing like Hubert's "directors" (we will discuss them in Chapter 7). I explained to him that many beings coordinated the construction of the pyramids at Giza. Some groups were simply extraterrestrials like Hubert's directors who didn't have the luxury of anti-gravity devices. They didn't complete these pyramids, and came and went several times during the construction phases.

Much of the real work on these pyramids was completed under the direction of the time travelers, who intervened when the directors and other non-time-traveler aliens abandoned the project. This seemed to satisfy Roger's curiosity.

His next past life regression also illustrated his natural flair for building, but was even more unusual. It seemed that around 3,500 years ago Roger was a type of freelance builder in the Middle East. He was a Mason and studied the Mysteries, but appeared to have learned his lesson and kept these secrets to himself, or discussed them within the inner circle of Masons.

One day, while working on a project, Roger was abducted in broad daylight by a beam of light from the same craft that had abducted him in 1983 and in ancient Egypt. The same time travelers informed Roger that he was to accompany them to a very special building site.

When they arrived and beamed Roger down to this site, he was amazed. What he saw was a large circle surrounding a semicircle of stones. He was in Stonehenge, England!

While getting his bearings in this new land, Roger was taken on board the spaceship several times and examined. He had several conferences alone with the human time traveler and was briefed about this project.

Roger, along with several other builders and less noteworthy workers, was to construct a structure that would function as an ancient airport for extraterrestrial crafts and an observatory to chart the movements of the planets, functioning as a type of astronomical calendar, with the huge stones serving as markers in the cyclical movements of the moon, sun, and stars.

It appeared to be a training lab for extraterrestrials while away from their planet. The time traveler explained to Roger that our species at first required the intervention of these aliens to facilitate our intellectual and biological evolution.

The chrononauts repaid this debt by assisting these aliens in their quest at times far in the distant past. Roger was not quite sure he understood everything, but he felt reasonably safe and promised to do his best.

Moving these huge stones required the use of several of the same antimatter flying vehicles Roger had observed in ancient Egypt. His work went well and he was again rewarded for his skill with food delicacies and anything else he desired.

Roger was alone again in this past life, but that didn't seem to matter. He did his job and recalled several more visits to the time travelers' spaceship during that lifetime. From the ground this craft sometimes appeared as a light green, luminous, disc-shaped object.

What was interesting in Roger's case so far was an external involvement, not only with these same time travelers, but with Masonry (Mystery Schools) and building in general, something in which he excelled.

The actual construction of Stonehenge took place in three phases, according to archaeologists. In phase 1, about 3100 B.C., a circular earthwork ditch about 320 feet in diameter was excavated. This ditch was 20 feet wide and 4.5 to 7 feet deep. Two parallel entry stones were erected on the northeast of the circle. One of these, called the Slaughter Stone, survives today.

A second phase of construction began around 2100 B.C., during which 80 bluestone pillars weighing 4 tons each were erected to form two concentric circles that were never completed. The entranceway of these stones was aligned with the sunrise at the summer solstice.

The final phase began around 1550 B.C., and this is the part that Roger worked on. A horseshoe of dressed bluestones set close together, and covered by a stone lintel, alternated with pillars. Many of the large stones had to be transported from the Marlborough Downs, about twenty miles north. This is where the anti-gravity flying cars came in handy.

The remaining bluestones, forming a circle around the sarsen horseshoe of stones, were set as a circle of pillars and aligned with stone lintels.

Attempts by scholars to link Stonehenge to Egyptians, Phoenicians, Greeks, Romans, Druids, Danes, Buddhists, Hindus, and Mayans have all failed to prove their case. Roger's second past life suggests very strongly that this megalith was built by the time travelers.

The last past life to which I regressed Roger took place in Paris during the Middle Ages. During the early 1200s, Roger was again a builder and a Mason. He lived with his wife and daughter in Paris, and was engaged in the construction of the Notre Dame Cathedral.

He describes some frustration in having to work around the remnants of ruins from a previous construction. This didn't appear to represent a major problem, and he continued on with his work.

Although married and the father of a bright and respectful daughter, Roger didn't appear to be fulfilled. He loved many aspects of his work and attended guild meetings. During a meeting he discussed metaphysics and practiced many techniques to travel out of the body and learn about the universe.

Roger wasn't quite happy and tended to drink too much at times. He would get into fights with his wife and even lose his temper with his loving daughter. The precise reason for his dissatisfaction was simply unknown.

He worked on Notre Dame for many years. The work was tedious, but Roger was a skillful builder and took great pride in his work. The hours were long and there were no vacations.

One day Roger just wandered off the job site and decided to take the afternoon off. He didn't get very far, as a beam of light transported him on board the time traveler ship. It was here that Roger went through the usual tests and spiritual enhancement training.

The abduction was one of several that occurred to Roger during the next two months or so. After each encounter he at first felt disoriented, but soon began to develop a more spiritual purpose in life. This was not an easy condition to maintain. He slipped back into old dysfunctional behaviors several times.

During the past life in medieval France, Roger had no memories of his abductions. He couldn't relay this experience to his fellow Masons, who were, ironically, the only people he knew that could possibly understand this phenomenon.

As an interesting aside, the Notre Dame Cathedral was built on the ruins of two earlier churches. The bishop of Paris, Maurice de Sully, began this project in 1160. Most of the renovations on this structure were completed by 1250. Porches, chapels and other embellishments were added over the next 100 years.

At the end of these past life regressions Roger was finally getting the big picture. He easily saw why his life changed so dramatically in 1983. Roger could see the pattern of his life's work as a real estate developer who liked to build things himself every now and then. He found a logical explanation for his interests in metaphysics, and the reason the "Hubert Meets Aliens in Egypt" chapter in *Past Lives—Future Lives* bothered him so much.

There were no real problems for me to assist Roger in solving. His issue was an existential one. Now he knew about his abductions and spiritual training by the same time travelers in three of his past lives. Roger came to me in quest of answers and he found them. Roger's life and lives were an example of a successful time traveler experiment.

The abductions of Wendy

When Wendy came to my office in 1994 she reported classic "missing time" episodes characteristic of UFO abductions. This twenty-seven-year-old graphic designer had seen me on the 11:00 P.M. news following my CBS movie, *Search for Grace*.[1] Her chief clinical problems were overeating and depression.

I conducted a past life regression on that three-minute news segment, and Wendy felt confident I could assist her in recalling what occurred during these missing time experiences, the last of which took place in January of 1994.

In hypnosis Wendy described hearing in her bedroom one night a low buzzing sound that became louder and was soon accompanied by a

---

1   This television movie was based on one of the most documented cases of reincarnations of this century, as described in my book reprinted by Llewellyn, *The Search for Grace: The True Story of Murder and Reincarnation* (St. Paul: Llewellyn, 1997).

zapping sensation, as if she was being electrocuted. The buzz transformed into a violent sucking of air and subsequently was replaced by a siren-pitched wail so loud that she thought her head was going to explode.

Nothing appeared disturbed in her room. She lived alone in a rented home in Los Angeles and had no previous interest or belief in UFOs. Suddenly, a crackling slice of light burst from the ceiling and temporarily blinded her. Her body became rigid and she literally floated out of her window enveloped by this blinding light. A large white, luminous, saucer-shaped UFO was beaming her up to it with a golden light.

The next thing she could recall in hypnosis was a laboratory occupied by several gray aliens with the classic, almond-shaped black eyes. The one closest to her, who appeared to be their leader, wore a white robe dotted with brilliant gold buttons down the middle. This being also wore a shining flaxen sash wrapped around the waist, with braided ropes hanging down the front.

The other aliens wore jumpsuit uniforms and appeared to be subservient to this being. All communication was by telepathy. Wendy felt comfortable enough to ask them questions. The leader didn't say much, but what he did tell Wendy truly shocked her.

This leader alien told Wendy that they would be removing some of her eggs as part of their reproductive experiments. These beings were nearly sterile and human eggs and sperm were necessary for their survival. Somehow Wendy was now dressed in a white garment (she could not recall removing her clothes and changing into this attire) and lying on an examination table.

The leader alien also telepathically communicated to Wendy not to exhibit anxiety or fear and that she would shortly learn things that would benefit her greatly. During the procedures Wendy drifted from a semiconscious state to complete unconsciousness.

Her body felt numb and occasionally a static electricity-like sensation spread from her head to her toes. Samples were taken from her hair and nails. Just prior to these procedures she was given a multicolored liquid to drink and special lights were beamed all along her body.

The leader alien stood very close to her throughout the procedure, telepathically comforting and reassuring her that all would be fine. One of the procedures consisted of inserting a long tube through her navel. This did not cause pain, and Wendy became unconscious the moment she observed this.

Following the procedures Wendy found herself dressed in her regular clothes and sitting in a conference room. There was an unusual looking series of devices in front of her, and several other unoccupied chairs in this room. Three people entered this conference room, two military officers and a tall, blonde human with deep, blue eyes—he was wearing a long white robe.

The military officers identified themselves as doctors, one a psychiatrist and the other a physicist. They explained to her that this experiment was being conducted in cooperation with beings whose sole purpose was to help her.

Wendy never had trusted government spokespeople, especially military ones. She appeared quite uneasy until the tall, blonde human in the white robe telepathically communicated with her. He informed Wendy that he came from more than 1,200 years in her future, to assist in the technological development of our society.

Secondarily, he was here to train Wendy in her own spiritual growth. When she asked him point blank why he should care about her, he smiled and said, "You will soon see the significance of these events." Wendy immediately felt a surge of love and compassion emanating from this time traveler, and she calmed down.

Next, a hologram appeared on the conference table, produced by the odd-looking machines in front of her. The scene depicted Wendy at about sixteen years of age, being taken to this same military installation where a fetus was removed from her womb with a long metal tube-like instrument. The fetus was then placed in a special jar filled with liquid.

Wendy later reported to me that when she was sixteen she was diagnosed as being pregnant, even though she was a virgin and her hymen was intact. Her gynecologist was quite puzzled about her condition. The doctor was even more surprised when this fetus mysteriously disappeared three weeks later, with Wendy's hymen still intact.

After this hologram scene ended, Wendy was told by the time traveler that the aliens did originate from his time period, but were working under his direction. He also related to her that he and his colleagues have been both experimenting with our race and assisting us in our spiritual growth throughout our civilization's history, and long before we lived in organized groups.

The time traveler specifically pointed out that he and his group of futuristic aliens were working in collusion with our government in exchange for advanced technology. She was not to be concerned about their presence. The last thing he mentioned to her was that he and his team had taken egg samples from her and worked with her in several of her past lives! This shocked Wendy, but soon she felt the love and compassion again being directed at her by the chrononaut.

A device was placed about three feet above Wendy's head, shining a multicolored light down on the top of her head. This had the effect of calming her and making her feel very disoriented, but at peace.

Following this procedure she was shown another hologram depicting one of her past lives at the end of the 1500s in England. During this past life Wendy was a peasant girl, working as a waitress in a tavern.

She had a simple life, but noted how unhappy she really was. Although as this waitress Wendy presented a positive and social demeanor to the customers, personally she was miserable. As she viewed this hologram, Wendy could sense that the time traveler was saddened by this scene.

On several occasions during this reenactment of her English life, Wendy saw herself being beamed aboard a spaceship and examined by the same time travelers. The equipment was a little different, but most of the technology looked similar to what she remembered in the military installation's examination and treatment room she had just come from.

One thing that she especially noted was that during this English past life a helmet was placed on her head while she was on the craft, apparently tapping into and recording her memories. The blonde time traveler was there, conscientiously recording and storing this data.

Following this a hologram showing Wendy as a cavegirl about fifteen years of age was presented. In this primitive life she lived in a cave with her parents and a younger brother. When her parents were killed in an attack by a saber-toothed tiger, Wendy and her brother had to survive on their own.

She was shown several abduction scenes from that life depicting eggs being removed from her womb, and subsequent exposure to the helmet and light beam treatments. The time traveler informed Wendy that this cavegirl life was the result of a genetic experiment and took place about two million years ago.

Subsequent research revealed that the saber-toothed tiger was an extinct cat that lived approximately thirty million years ago. It became extinct in the Pleistocene epoch, about one million years B.C. One genus, *Smilodan*, about the size of a modern-day tiger, lived during the Pleistocene period. It had a long upper canine tooth that it used to pierce the thick hide of its prey. It would not be out of character for this animal to hunt humans.

Another hologram illustrated a recurrent pattern of overeating, showing Wendy in ancient Rome as the barren wife of a soldier. Eating was her only solace, and as the years went by while her husband was away on military campaigns she progressively became obese.

Beginning in her childhood during this Roman life, Wendy was abducted several times by the time travelers and underwent the usual procedures. This was not a happy life. Finally, she was informed of her husband's death in a battle, and took her own life by drinking poison.

Medieval Germany was the scene of Wendy's past life as a nun in a convent. Again, she did not have children and apparently that added to her depression in that life. Her days were spent performing menial functions, while her evenings were occupied with study and contemplation. To a certain degree she enjoyed a spiritual orientation, but on the whole this was not a satisfying experience.

Holographic scenes showed many abductions by the time travelers. They focused more on her spiritual development during her life as a nun, in that egg samples were not taken although other tests were conducted.

What was interesting to note is that during each of these holographic time presentations the time traveler appeared to be more and more compassionate toward Wendy. It was as if he had a personal stake in her growth.

The last hologram Wendy viewed showed her in her current life, approximately eighteen months in the future (around December 1995) becoming involved in a relationship with a man with red hair and driving a white Corvette. This meant nothing to her at the time.

Before Wendy was returned to her apartment, the military doctors left the room and the time traveler and Wendy were alone for a short talk. He informed Wendy that she wouldn't remember these events for now, but eventually she would recall them.

He then explained his personal interest in her, leaving Wendy speechless. This time traveler is Wendy's great-great-great-grandson! He specifically requested this assignment to personally work with his ancestor.

Following this talk Wendy was returned to her apartment. Because she was unconscious she couldn't relate exactly how this happened. The next thing she reported was being back in her bedroom, somewhat sore and with a headache.

Wendy made great progress in overcoming her compulsive overeating and depression in the weeks that followed. One unusual thing she reported was the occasional presence of unmarked black helicopters over her apartment and on the freeway when she drove to and from work.

For those of you that think this government collusion with the time travelers is merely an Oliver Stone conspiracy fantasy, be aware that these unmarked helicopters are reported by UFO abductees.[2] Could these be the Men in Black we hear about? We will discuss these Men in Black in greater detail in Chapter 6.

Wendy called me in 1996 to update me on her case. She had lost thirty pounds and no longer suffered from depression. Around Christmas 1995 she met Frank, a red-haired, thirty-two-year-old businessman who drives a white Corvette. They are now engaged. Some day one of Wendy's progeny is going to give birth to a time traveler.

---

2   Gray Barker, *They Knew Too Much About Flying Saucers* (New York: University Books, 1956).

Chapter 5

Time travelers as guardian angels

Biblical scholars refer to the Old Testament's Sons of Gods as celestial beings or angels. These "giants" apparently fell from the sky. There are many references to them interbreeding with the ancients. *Nephilum* is the Hebrew word for giants, and literally means "fallen-down ones."

Jewish scriptures name these angels Avim, Anakim, Zamzummin, Rephaim, Emin, and Horim,[1] portraying them as "mighty men which were of old, men of renown."[2] These ancient angels were most probably time travelers.

The demigods of Greek mythology have a similar origin. We also find many references to sexual contact between humans and other beings throughout the Middle Ages. The female succubi and male incubi were popular in Medieval days, but their history dates much further back into ancient times.

---

1 Genesis 14:5, 15:19-21; Numbers 13:23; Deuteronomy 2:10, 20, 21.
2 Genesis 6:4.

In this chapter we will see how some angelic encounters are nothing more than time travelers assisting us in our hour of need. Notice that I say "some encounters." My book *Soul Healing* (Llewellyn Publications, 1996), depicts examples of angelic interventions which I personally feel may very well be due to perfect beings.

I truly feel we were not meant to suffer in life. Recent surveys show that more than two-thirds of Americans believe in angels. About one in ten has had personal encounters with these messengers of love.

There are thousands of reports every year from people seeing "glowing beings of light" that assist them in time of need. One theory states that from the moment you were born, your Guardian Angels have been by your side, wishing only to shield you from harm and offer you guidance. Have we not all had dreams of angelic beings?

Angels have made the covers of *Time* and *Newsweek,* and have been featured on the major television networks. Harvard Divinity School and Boston College offer special classes in Angelology, teaching that these spirits move between the layers of the universe to deliver messages from heaven to help us ascend. Does this mechanism remind you of hyperspace?

I will present several cases shortly that demonstrate how some of these angelic experiences are in reality our friendly time travelers. We have thoroughly discussed hyperspace in chapter 3. In that chapter I pointed out how the other dimensions beyond our fourth dimension are characterized by a higher vibrational rate of energy. Time travelers from these levels could actually be walking among us now—completely invisible to us. They would become visible only if their vibrational rate were suddenly slowed down. They could appear to us whenever they wanted to, or remain invisible.

Frequently reported also are the spirit guides or Masters seen by people who survive a near-death experience (NDE). Could not some of these "angels" be time travelers on a higher dimension in hyperspace?

Even the very insights we receive that can turn our lives around or save a life can be explained by time traveler communication. Our intuition seems to operate instantaneously, on a higher wavelength. This may explain why intuition has the power to grasp complex realities beyond the range of our everyday thought.

One of the ways I perceive time travelers communicating with us to assist us in our intellectual and spiritual development is through automatic writing. Throughout history there have been many examples of automatic writing leading to a compilation of previously unknown knowledge that often surpasses the level of humanity's learning at the time it is written.

We can look to the origin of religious scriptures, especially the Koran, which was the result of direct "angelic" communication. The Theosophical movement, the Mystery Schools, Freemasonry, the Rosicrucians, the writings of Thomas Jefferson, Rousseau, Leonardo Da Vinci, Thomas Edison, Benjamin Franklin, and a host of others suggest something beyond normal acquisition of knowledge.

A time traveler stops a bullet

Drive-by shootings are unfortunately common in most cities in America today. In 1991 one of my patients was walking down a street in a busy downtown area of Miami, on her way to do some clothes shopping for an upcoming job interview.

Suddenly a car came screeching by right in front of her. In it were a group of teenage boys with some sort of automatic weapons, threatening to shoot her and several other people.

Just as they were about to shoot her and the other pedestrians, she froze and doesn't recall what happened next. Her watch stopped and when she awoke she just continued on her way to the clothing store. This was only one of many missing time episodes in her life.

After the job interview a week later she sat down at her desk in her apartment to write a letter to her brother who lived out of state. Instead of composing her thoughts, her right hand wrote a note, as if by itself, stating that she would get the job she applied for and that her guardian angel had saved her life outside the clothing store the previous week.

When I regressed her, she reported an abduction on board a time traveler craft, as I described in the previous chapter. A white-robed human chrononaut showed her a hologram depicting that drive-by shooting.

In this reenactment, a luminous red ball was projected from a small box on the jumpsuit of an alien-looking chrononaut that placed the teenage gang and everyone else on the street in suspended animation. The time traveler then made the automatic weapon nonfunctional and beamed back up into the craft.

What makes these and other reports more credible is the fact that the paradigms I am presenting are unique. She couldn't have read about these time travelers in a book or other printed media. As an aside, she did get the job she applied for as predicted by the time traveler.

A time traveler "doctor" cures cancer

One hypnotic age regression I conducted a few years ago illustrated the healing powers of those light beams I keep describing. This middle-aged female patient had an incurable case of cancer in her pancreas that was about to take her life. Eileen's stay in the hospital was not a happy one.

A new young doctor came into her room. He told her he was a resident, and that he would be conducting an examination for the purpose of recommending her for chemotherapy. Eileen thought this rather odd, since her regular oncologist had clearly stated there was nothing more he could do for her.

Eileen consented to the exam and the young, blonde-haired doctor with piercing blue eyes proceeded to shine a pen flashlight emitting a blue/red light at the area of her pancreas. When she asked why he was doing that, he simply smiled.

The young doctor left and Eileen discussed this unusual visit with her oncologist the following day when he was running a series of routine tests before sending her home. She left the hospital and received a most unusual call from her own doctor a few days later.

Her oncologist told Eileen that her tests showed no cancer was present. He was sure it had to be an error, and apologetically requested that Eileen return to the hospital for more tests. She did and a complete series of tests revealed she was cancer free.

An abduction she had some time later confirmed the fact that a time traveler had posed as the young resident. He telepathically told her that it wasn't her time yet and that occasionally these chrononauts save the lives of people they observe and empower.

A time traveler saves a mountain climber

A male patient from the Midwest was vacationing in Switzerland and nearly died in a mountain-climbing accident. He was climbing a steep mountain alone one windy afternoon, and lost his balance.

Instead of falling to his death, he felt his body being caught by a luminous being. He could see this tall, blonde time traveler holding him until they both reached the ground safely. Then the mysterious being pushed a button on his white robe and disappeared.

In my office we finally unraveled this mystery. This time traveler originated from about 3,000 years in our future. By that time dematerialization and rematerialization will be perfected. Whether this chrononaut had mastered hyperspace, or simply reassembled his atoms, I do not know.

What I am aware of is that he saved my patient's life by functioning as an angel. This category of time travelers do not travel by way of spaceships. They simply beam themselves anywhere they want to go.

The bulletproof time traveler

I don't know why gangs like to hang out in alleys, but they do. One of my younger male patients (age eighteen) was a member of a gang in Los Angeles. He had second thoughts about his involvement with their nefarious activities, but didn't have the courage to quit this substitute family.

One of their activities consisted of beating up rival gangs, usually in an alley. On a warm Friday evening he found himself in such an alley preparing for a "rumble." One member of the other gang pulled out a gun and aimed it at my patient.

Before the gun could go off, a swirling blue and lavender cloud surrounded this potential killer. The luminous figure of a human time traveler in a white robe stood between the gunman and my young patient. The gun went off, but the bullets seemed to enter the chrononaut's body and disappear from sight.

While this was going on, everyone else was placed in a state of suspended animation. When the swirling cloud evaporated the time traveler was gone and every gang member regained consciousness. They just dispersed.

The following day my patient withdrew from the gang and his whole life changed. He began working to help support his poor family, and became far more spiritual than he had ever been before. I was only able to obtain this information during a hypnotic regression, when an abduction on board a time traveler vessel and a holographic depiction of this event ensued.

A time traveler becomes an angel in a past life

In the previous chapter I described how time travelers follow us from lifetime to lifetime to assist our growth on many levels. It should not come as a surprise that they can function as guardian angels during these previous incarnations.

In a past life on the American western frontier during the early 1800s my male patient, Carl, was the young husband of Sarah. They lived in a log cabin and life was hard. "Bob" was a farmer. Sarah was a devout Christian and never lost her faith in God, no matter how harshly the universe treated her and her family.

Sarah had two infant children and loved her young family very much. The main problems she and her family faced were providing enough food to live on and protecting themselves from the Indians.

Bob was a good man and worked hard. He did his best to provide for his family, but was quickly losing his faith in God. No matter what he did or how hard he worked, it was just barely enough for survival. Bob wanted to believe in a higher power, as Sarah did, but he couldn't rationalize this concept in relationship to his life's experience.

It was as if he needed some test to demonstrate a purpose to his being beyond mere labor and physical drudgery. The universe, by way of the time travelers, was about to do just that.

One night Bob and Sarah heard some noise outside their cabin. It sounded like a group of men running around the building. When Bob stepped outside he saw about fifty or more savage Indians carrying fiery torches and surrounding his home.

There wasn't anything he could do to prevent a massacre. Bob knew that these warriors would kill him, then his children, rape Sarah, and finally take her life. Then they would burn down his cabin. He just stood there and prayed to God for help.

Suddenly, a tall, luminous, white-robed, blonde time traveler descended from the air above the cabin and stood just in front of Bob. This chrononaut did not say anything, he just stood there looking confident and luminescent.

The effect was instantaneous. The Indians dropped their torches and bowed to the time traveler as if he were a god. As the time traveler approached Bob, he telepathically informed Bob who he was and told him not to be afraid. Bob thanked him as he watched the Indians run away.

From that day on Bob regained his faith in God. His life improved dramatically and he never saw Indians again. The farm produced abundant crops, and Bob watched his children grow up to become model citizens.

In his present life as Carl, my patient did not have to be abducted to obtain knowledge of his time traveler. He has reported no missing time episodes, and my superconscious mind tap technique confirmed that Carl had not been abducted in his present incarnation.

My conclusion concerning the time travelers as guardian angels is that they definitely have played a part in our image of angels. The luminous appearance they take may explain the halos often appearing in Medieval and Renaissance art depicting Madonnas and angels.

I don't think all angelic cases are time traveler encounters, just some of them. These time travelers are keeping a watchful eye over us. They protect us, as well as train us in spiritual unfolding techniques.

Chapter 6

Men in black

One of the most controversial and misunderstood elements of abductions and UFO history are the Men in Black (MIB). The first step in comprehending this phenomenon is to put aside the 1997 feature film *Men In Black,* starring Tommy Lee Jones and Will Smith. Remember, this was comedy, not a docudrama.

Descriptions of these unusual men vary, but they do possess some common components. Among these characteristics are:

- They are robotic, similar to the Jack Webb character of *Dragnet* fame. Their voices sound mechanical and monotone-like.

- The men are dressed in black suits, and wear white shirts and black ties. They wear black hats, sunglasses, and thick-soled black shoes.

- Sinister looks are frequently reported. The men have been reported as appearing pale and bug-eyed. Many are reported to be Asian-looking, with dark skin.

- The men drive large black cars. We find Cadillacs (sometimes very old models) reported in the United States and Jaguars in Great Britain and on the European continent. The license plates are always phony.

- They may appear alone, but are usually seen in groups of two or three, with three being the most common.

- These men represent themselves to be government agents, but no agency acknowledges their existence.

- They use a flash gun, like those associated with cameras. Ironically, the 1997 movie *Men In Black* used this characteristic throughout the film. Their device had a red light that when flashed erased all a subject's memories permanently.

- Unusual electrical events accompany MIB sightings. Strange sounds are occasionally reported on telephone lines and other unexplained disturbances occur.

- Certain MIB appear ill after a short visit and request water to take a pill or salt! It's as if their energy has run down.

- MIB almost always attempt to silence witnesses to UFOs or other unusual phenomena.

- Some MIB are characterized as very tall, with unnaturally long fingers.

- Occasionally the insignia of a triangle with an eye in the center is seen on their clothes or car.

- Unmarked black helicopters are occasionally piloted by MIBs, and follow abductees for several months after their abductions.

- Some of these Men in Black appear quite efficient, while others act in a most incompetent fashion. For example, the latter type don't appear to comprehend how to use a ballpoint pen or other simple amenities of life in our time. Certain reports depict these MIB as having trouble walking and appearing disoriented when asked a simple question.

Men in Black have been reported since ancient times. I believe that many of these beings are time travelers from 1,000 to 3,000 years in our future. They may be completely human or hybrids; I do not have any reports of the future MIB being pure alien.

The Men in Black from about 1,000 years in our future are far less competent than their colleagues from further out in our future. They only exist in the first place as a concession by the time travelers to their secret alliance with our government, as I briefly discussed at the end of Chapter 5.

Since these Men in Black represent a form of future policemen, they are the least spiritually evolved examples of our future, and become the true time traveler's worst nightmare. While the time travelers I have previously described function to assist us in our spiritual growth, these MIBs' only purpose is to silence witnesses, preventing premature reports of these encounters by the public. This was all arranged through specific deals made between the United States government and the time travelers.

I should say at this point that other governments, both today and throughout ancient times, have made similar pacts, one reason the Mystery Schools functioned as they did. The secretive pattern of all governments throughout history mirrors this behavior. In ancient times some of these Men in Black killed those who attempted to disseminate their encounters with time travelers to others. Foul play is suspected today in certain unusual but convenient deaths and disappearances of UFO investigators and witnesses.

The early history of MIB shows their close association with black magic. Macumba is a religion of Africans who were transplanted to the New World. Two spirits known as Omulu ("Old Black") and Exu or Elegba equate with MIB. Omulu dresses in a black robe and lends his support to the devil. Exu is in charge of the force of *Quimbanda*, or black magic, and actually is the devil. He wears a top hat and a black suit.

We find "the Black Man" during the Middle Ages as the Devil or Satan. He traveled in the form of a black cat, dog, wolf, or other creature. The grimoires of the time described him wearing black. Even the Black Mass had "black priests."

Hilary Evans describes the confession in 1603 in southern France of a young man who was accused of kidnapping and eating a child! He declared that the Lord of the Forest, a tall dark man who wore a black outfit and rode a black horse, ordered him to do so.[1]

Anthropologist Margaret Murray described a testimony given at the trial of a witch as follows:

> The witch mark is sometimes like a blew spot, or a little tate, or reid spots, like a flea biting; sometimes also the flesh is sunk in, and hollow, and this is put in secret places, as among the hair of the head, or eye-brows, within the lips, under the arm-pits, and in the most secret parts of the body.

We can draw a parallel to the "scooped-out" scars and other markings that are commonly reported by UFO abductees with these "Devils marks" and "nips."[2]

A British newspaper, the *Barmouth Advertiser,* on March 30, 1905 reported, "An exceptionally intelligent young woman of the peasant class was visited three nights in succession by a Man in Black. This figure has delivered a message to the girl which she is frightened to relate." What is interesting about the winter of 1904–1905 in Britain was the many unusual happenings that occurred, including four spontaneous human combustion cases, poltergeist phenomena, and other strange events.

Jerome Clark reported an MIB that same winter in Wales:

> During [religious revivalist] Mrs. Jones' visit to Bryncrug, in the neighborhood of Towyn, a similar apparition was seen from different standpoints, but simultaneously by (a) a local

---

1 H. Evans *Mysteries of Mind, Space & Time* (Westport, CT: Orbis, 1992).
2 J. Clark, "Mystery Lights, Fires and Mass Hysteria," *Nexus New Times,* 2 (25), May 1995.

professional man and (b) a gentleman farmer of good standing. The former, startled, uttered an involuntary prayer. Immediately one of Mrs. Jones' mysterious "Lights" appeared above, a white ray darting from [it] which pierced the figure, which thereupon vanished.[3]

A futuristic species of black magicians called the *zobop* terrorized the people of Haiti during the 1940s. They drove around in black cars called *motor-zobop* or *tiger-cars,* which disabled abductees by sending out a bluish beam of light.

We have seen some nefarious examples of MIB. Now let us look at positive effects these characters have had on history. Manly P. Hall reports that an MIB assisted in the designing of the Colonial flag in 1775 America:

> By something more than a mere coincidence the committee appointed by the Colonial Congress to design a flag accepted an invitation to be guests, while in Cambridge, of the same family with which the Professor was staying. It was here that General Washington joined them for the purpose of deciding upon a fitting emblem. By the signs which passed between them it was evident that both General Washington and Doctor Franklin recognized the Professor, and by unanimous approval he was invited to become an active member of the committee. During the proceedings which followed, the Professor was treated with the most profound respect and all of his suggestions immediately acted upon. He submitted a pattern which he considered symbolically appropriate for the new flag, and this was unhesitatingly accepted by the other six members of the committee, who voted that the arrangement suggested by the Professor be forthwith adopted. After the episode of the flag the professor quietly vanished, and nothing further is known concerning him.[4]

Thomas Jefferson had an encounter with a mysterious dark-skinned man dressed in a black cape, who handed him the original design for the

---

3 Ibid.

4 Manly P. Hall, *The Secret Teachings of All Ages* (Los Angeles: The Philosophical Research Society, Inc., 1977).

Great Seal of the United States. John Keel describes the seal as a reproduction of the lost Arabian city of Petra, once inhabited by an ancient race known as Nabataeans. These people reportedly were a highly advanced civilization.[5]

There are two forces operating in our universe, according to occult tradition. One is called the White Brotherhood; these souls are committed to the perfection of humanity. The other force is known as the Black Lodge or Black Brotherhood. This latter group attempts to repress our growth spiritually.

Some look upon the White Brotherhood as angels and the Black Brotherhood as demons, but I prefer to view them as time travelers and MIB, respectively. I do not consider the MIB evil or demonic, just hard-nosed repressive cops, "doing their job."

We can see how the MIB act to stifle our spiritual growth with their threats and harassing tactics. By silencing witnesses and instilling fear, they work in a way completely antagonistic to the time travelers. Apparently this doesn't bother the governments that have allowed them on the scene throughout history since biblical times.

The first modern MIB report

On June 21, 1947, a military man named Harold Dahl took photos of six UFOs flying above Puget Sound in Washington State. He described his sightings as follows:

> In describing the aircraft I would say they were at least one hundred feet in diameter. Each had a hole in the center, approximately twenty-five feet in diameter. They were all a sort of shell-like gold and silver color. Their surface seemed of metal and appeared to be burled because when the light shone on them through the clouds they were brilliant, not all one brilliance, but many brilliances, something like a Buick dashboard. All of the aircraft seemed to have large portholes equally spaced around the outside of their doughnut exterior. These portholes

---

5   T. G. Beckley, *The UFO Silencers* (New Brunswick, NJ: Inner Light, 1990).

were from five to six feet in diameter and were round. They also appeared to have a dark, circular, continuous window on the inside and bottom of their doughnut shape as thought it were an observation window.[6]

This sighting occurred thirteen days before the UFO crashes at Roswell and Corona, and three days prior to the Kenneth Arnold UFO sighting that ushered in the modern wave of UFO reports. One of the six UFOs sighted by Dahl exploded, and Dahl collected samples of the metal.

Later that morning an MIB contacted Dahl and had breakfast with him at a local restaurant. After describing the UFO sighting and explosion in detail, this MIB threatened Dahl and his family if he ever divulged the details of the encounter. Dahl ignored this threat; when he had the film developed, the pictures were mysteriously fogged and later "misplaced."

Eventually reporter Kenneth Arnold was sent to investigate this sighting at Maury Island, Washington. Arnold had just witnessed his own UFO sighting and labeled them "flying saucers." When Arnold finally inspected the metal scraps and lava rocks given to him by Dahl's superior officer Crisman, discrepancies were observed from Dahl's original description of them.

The MIB had apparently gotten to Crisman, as Crisman wanted Military Intelligence to take charge of the investigation. Two Army Air Corps officers (First Lieutenant Frank M. Brown and Captain William L. Davidson of Army Intelligence) were killed when their plane carrying samples of this UFO debris crashed on August 1.

Kenneth Arnold had an attempt made on his life two days later while piloting his plane back to Boise, Idaho. He discovered that someone had shut off the fuel valve. Other deaths included Paul Lance, a reporter for the *Tacoma Times,* who helped Arnold with his investigation, and a United Press reporter at Tacoma.

---

6   K. Arnold and P. Ray, *The Coming of the Saucers* (Amherst, WI: self-published manuscript, 1952).

The *Tacoma Times* ran the following story headlined "Sabotage Hinted in Crash of Army Bomber at Kelso":

> The mystery of the "Flying Saucers" soared into prominence again Saturday when the Tacoma Times was informed that the crash Friday of an army plane at Kelso may have been caused by sabotage.
>
> The *Times'* informant, in a series of mysterious phone calls, reported that the ship had been sabotaged "or shot down" to prevent shipment of flying disk fragments to Hamilton Field, California, for analysis.
>
> The disk parts were said by the informant to be those from one of the mysterious platters which plunged to Earth on Maury Island recently.
>
> Lending substance to the caller's story is the fact that TWELVE HOURS BEFORE THE ARMY RELEASED OFFICIAL IDENTIFICATION, he correctly identified the dead in the crash to be Captain William L. Davidson, pilot, and First Lieutenant Frank M. Brown.[7]

It is interesting that the *Tacoma Times* went out of business shortly thereafter.

Albert K. Bender and the MIB

One of the most well known and nefarious MIB stories concerns Albert K. Bender. This thirty-one-year old Bridgeport, Connecticut, resident formed the International Flying Saucer Bureau (IFSB) in 1953 and began publishing *Space Review.*

In the October 1953 issue of *Space Review* two startling announcements appeared:

> LATE BULLETIN: A source which the IFSB considers very reliable has informed us that the investigation of the flying saucer mystery and the solution is approaching its final stages. This same source to whom we had referred data, which had come

---

7   B. Burden, "MIBs and the Intelligence Community." *Awareness,* Spring, 1980.

into our possession, suggested that it was not the proper method and time to publish the data in *Space Review*.

The mystery of the flying saucers is no longer a mystery. The source is already known, but any information about this is being withheld by order from a higher source. We would like to print the full story in *Space Review*, but because of the nature of the information we are very sorry that we have been advised in the negative. We advise those engaged in saucer work to please be very cautious.[8]

This was the last issue of *Space Review*. Bender closed down the IFSB and briefly described his MIB contact with a local newspaper. When asked whether they were FBI agents, Bender responded that they were "from another branch."

The ufologist Gray Barker first publicized Bender's story in *Fate* magazine. What he uncovered was that IFSB informants and researchers were hired away into top security government positions, so they could no longer discuss their previous findings due to national security.

One of the IFSB's researchers, Dominick C. Lucchesi, recorded a message that was discovered by Barker. It said:

Three men had visited him [Bender], and in effect shut him up completely as far as saucer investigation is concerned.

Now the way I hear it, Al [Bender] had run across something important during his study of the saucer mystery. . . . He had run across the secret unexpectedly while going through all this [IFSB] material)....

The remaining copies of *Space Review*... had been confiscated. ...He [Bender] was pledged to secrecy, on his honor as an American citizen not to speak about the actual thing that he knew.[9]

Bender's response to his MIB visit was that the MIB revealed to him the secret of the UFOs and threatened him with prison if he let the information out. A three-day illness followed this encounter. One of

8   G. Barker, *They Knew Too Much About Flying Saucers* (New York: University Books, 1956).
9   Barker, op. cit.

Bender's Australian colleagues, the head of the Australian Flying Saucer Bureau, had a similar MIB visit.

This man, Edgar Jarrold, was followed by a black car, experienced poltergeist phenomena, was knocked down a flight of stairs by an unknown force, and kept getting unusual phone calls. Jarrold dropped out of the field and soon was reported to have mysteriously disappeared.

Gray Barker's 1956 bestseller, *They Knew Too Much About Flying Saucers*, focused on the Bender case and others like it involving MIB encounters. In 1962 Barker published Bender's book titled *Flying Saucers and the Three Men*,[10] continuing to foster the public interest in MIB engendered by Barker's 1956 book. Bender, although still alive in 1997, refuses to discuss his MIB experiences.

One final note about Bender's IFSB is that it was involved in rather sophisticated UFO analysis of sightings, and attempted to determine the base of origin. It is not difficult to see how this would draw to Bender the attention of the FBI, CIA, and Air Force.

"Make him look like a nut"

An engineer named Rex Ball accidentally wandered into an underground base in Georgia in 1940. A large number of small Asian-looking men in coveralls and American military officers were manning this base. An officer who spotted Ball called out to the others, "Make him look like a nut!" This appeared to be a standard operation by the government to make the witness of an MIB or UFO incident look foolish ("like a nut"). Ball awoke in a field, confused and unsure of whether he had dreamed the entire incident.[11]

---

10 A. K. Bender, *Flying Saucers and the Three Men* (Clarksburg, WV: Saucerian Books, 1962).

11 J. Keel, *The Mothman Prophecies* (Avondale Estates, GA: Illumi Net Press, 1991).

Malcolm X and an MIB

While Malcolm X was in Norfolk Prison Colony in 1949, he suddenly saw in his cell a man encircled by light sitting in a chair. This man had light brown skin, oily black hair, and appeared to be of Asian descent.

After exchanging stares, the odd-looking man vanished. The effect on Malcolm X was great. He thought he had received a visitation from Master Wallace Fard Muhammad, the founder of the Nation of Islam and the entity who revealed his mystical secrets to Elijah Muhammad.

At this juncture I cannot say whether Malcolm X's visitor was a regular time traveler or an MIB. What is interesting to note is that both Fard and Elijah Muhammad were initiates in High Degree Prince Hall Freemasonry.

In November 1961, Paul Miller, on a hunting trip with three friends, observed a "luminous silo" landing in a field nearby. Miller shot one of the two humanoid-looking creatures that emerged from the craft. On their return home these hunters experienced a missing time episode of about three hours.

Miller worked in a local Air Force base and met the following morning with three MIB claiming to be government agents. When Miller inquired how these agents knew about his involvement with this CE, the MIB responded that they had "a report."

These MIB showed an intimate knowledge of Miller's past, and threatened him if he should discuss this incident with anyone else, especially the press. Miller was frightened and wouldn't discuss this event for several years.

California highway inspector Rex Heflin took some Polaroid photos of a UFO that was parked near the Santa Ana Freeway on August 3, 1965. An MIB later took three of the four original photos, stating he was from North American Air Defense Command. NORAD denied ever sending an investigator to this site.

Two years later Captain C. H. Edmonds of Space Systems Division, Systems Command of the Air Force, interviewed Heflin. Edmonds offered to return the photos, and seemed quite relieved when Heflin said it wasn't necessary.

Heflin later reported to the Condon committee that a car was parked across the street and "In the back seat could be seen a figure and a violet glow, which the witness attributed to instrument dials. He believed he was being photographed or recorded. In the meantime his FM multiplex radio was playing in the living room and during the questioning it made several loud, audible pops."[12]

Other MIB cases have involved glowing instruments. Some theorize that the reason these instruments weren't covered up had to do with heat diffusion experienced with the use of vacuum tube-based equipment. A check with the Air Force uncovered the fact that Captain Edmonds did not exist!

During the mid-1960s, while he was writing a UFO book titled *Uninvited Visitors,* author Ivan Sanderson noticed a car that kept driving back and forth past his New Jersey home. Investigation revealed that the license plate of this car simply did not exist.

Some time later two men dressed in Air Force uniforms came to Sanderson's home, but refused to produce identification. Sanderson forced them to leave by gunpoint, and later was informed by the Air Force that no such men were sent to his home. Strange electronic sounds were heard over Sanderson's telephone for several weeks following this incident.

A classic MIB incident was experienced by the family of Edward Christiansen while driving through Mayville, New Jersey, on November 22, 1967. A glowing white, green, and red sphere was observed making sharp turns and flying directly over their heads as they pulled off the Garden State Parkway.

When they returned to their home in Wildwood Crest, New Jersey, the Christiansens called the Air Force. Several officers questioned the family about this sighting. In January of the following year an odd-looking man visited the Christiansens, claiming to be from the Missing Heirs Bureau. He stated that Edward may have inherited a large sum of money. This man identified himself as "Tiny."

---

12 Beckley, op. cit.

Tiny was over six feet tall, weighed over 300 pounds, wore a Russian-style fur hat with a black visor and a long black coat made of material too thin for winter wear. His eyes bugged out, with one appearing to be a glass eye.

The Christiansens described Tiny's voice as a computer-like monotone, with clipped phrases. He wheezed as he spoke. Upon removing his coat they noticed a badge that appeared to have a large K with a small x alongside it. Numbers or letters surrounded this badge. Tiny quickly covered it up with his hand as he spoke to them.

When Tiny sat down the Christiansens noted his thick-soled black shoes, black socks and pants, and a green wire originating from one sock and running up his leg.

Tiny asked Edward several questions concerning his background, the scars on his body, and schools he attended. The MIB's face grew quite red, but when he took a yellow capsule with water, his face immediately returned to its normal pallor.

About forty-five minutes later Tiny left, driving off in a 1963 black Cadillac. A woman called the following morning from the Missing Heirs Bureau to report that they had located the correct Edward Christiansen.

At least twenty-two incidents of cattle mutilations were reported in Madison County, Montana, between June and October 1976. Hunters observed black unmarked helicopters in the vicinity of Red Mountain near Norris, Montana. Upon following one of these helicopters, a local hunter sighted seven MIB walking toward a hill. These men were Asian, spoke an unknown language, and fled into the chopper which immediately took off.

In Carlisle, England, the Templeton family was enjoying a picnic on May 24, 1964. James Templeton, the father, photographed his youngest daughter Elizabeth picking wildflowers. A seven-foot-tall man wearing a white spacesuit appeared on the developed film.

This photo was taken to the local police and eventually published in the *Cumberland News*. The newspaper contacted the Ministry of Defense and Templeton soon was approached by two strange men asking him to go to the site of the photo.

Templeton assumed they were from the Ministry of Defense (MOD) and accompanied them in their Jaguar. These men were dressed in black suits, did not give their names, quickly showed Templeton official-looking IDs, and called each other "9" and "11."

Upon interrogation at the site where the photos were taken, these MIB insisted that they knew the mysterious figure in the photo to be a passerby. Templeton stated that his family saw no one else there. An argument ensued and the MIB drove off in their Jaguar, leaving Templeton behind.[13]

A UFO researcher in Coventry, England named Brian Leatherley-Andrew reported the following incident in October 1968:

> I was by myself. Suddenly I noticed a man standing by the next-door garage. Nobody had been there before. His face was glowing orange and as I watched, the face changed to that of an old man before my eyes. You could not describe the first face in normal terms. It had eyes, nose, and mouth in the proper places but not of the shape that we associate with the human figure.[14]

Brian was so bothered by this and the subsequent problems with his telephone and threatening phone calls that he abandoned his interest in UFOs.

Dr. Herbert Hopkins, a UFO researcher from Orchard Beach, Maine reported a most unusual encounter with an MIB on the evening of September 11, 1976. A man claiming to be the vice president of the New Jersey UFO Research Organization (a non-existent group) telephoned Dr. Hopkins to discuss a case that Hopkins was investigating. The case involved the hypnotic regression of David Stephens to an abduction he had experienced.

Just moments after Hopkins agreed to meet this MIB, the man appeared on his front porch. No car was present and it was literally impossible for the stranger to have arrived so quickly from any nearby phone.

---

13 J. Clark, *The UFO Encyclopedia* (Detroit: Omnigraphics Inc., 1996).
14 J. Keel, *The Complete Guide to Mysterious Beings* (New York: Doubleday & Co., 1994).

When the stranger entered Hopkins' home, the doctor's dog ran into the closet to hide. The dog's reaction was completely out of character, as it was an excellent watchdog.

The MIB was attired entirely in black and wore suede gloves and a derby hat; there were no buttons on his jacket. He was completely bald, with no eyelashes or eyebrows. Although his lips were bright red, the color of his skin was reported as dead white, with an odd plastic-like texture.

The MIB's lips did not smile, or turn up or down; they simply appeared flat, like those on a dummy. The red color was due to poorly applied lipstick. Although the MIB's body moved, Hopkins never observed any head movements.

A monotone-like voice emanated from this MIB. He spoke English and was quite knowledgeable about the Stephens case. Hopkins described his speech as a "scanning speech." No phrases or sentences were spoken, just a sequence of evenly spaced words.

The next thing the MIB did was to inform Hopkins that he had a dime and a penny in his pocket (which was true). Hopkins was instructed to remove one of them and hold it in his open hand. The following took place next, as reported by Dr. Hopkins:

> It was a bright new copper penny, and I held it up in my fingers, but I was asked to hold it flat in the palm of my hand. I did so and looked at him, not knowing what to expect next. "Don't look at me, watch the coin," he said. And I did. It suddenly began to develop a silvery color—and the silver became blue, and then I had trouble focusing. I could focus on my hand perfectly well— that was my reference point—but the coin simply was gone. Not abruptly. It simply slowly dematerialized—it just wasn't there anymore. I didn't smell anything. I didn't feel anything. I didn't hear anything.
>
> I was just fascinated at that point. I was spellbound, and I knew something strange was happening in my hand, because I could feel the weight of the penny going away. I don't know how he did this. He didn't perform any hocus-pocus, he didn't move his hands in any way.[15]

15 S. Devney, "Beware of the Diabolical Men-in-Black!" *UFO Universe,* Summer 1989.

Following this demonstration, the MIB threatened Hopkins if he didn't destroy his tapes of Stephens' regressions, along with any other UFO research data he had. Then the MIB appeared to run out of energy and left.

Dr. Hopkins noted a bluish light in the driveway and a quick flash of light. The MIB vanished with this flash. Following this visit Hopkins erased his tapes and lost interest in UFO research.

It is quite obvious that these MIB reports test our belief in reality. Hyperspace models most certainly explain many of these occurrences, but what is reality? The late Michael Talbot said it well when he wrote:

> Are these other realities actually places as we conceive of them or do they exist within our heads? In the paradigm of reality offered by both mysticism and the new physics, such a question becomes meaningless....The universe itself is not a place in the paradigm of the new physics. As Don Juan warns, there is no world "out there," only a description of the world. With the advent of the participator principle [of physics] the entire matter-space-time continuum of the physical universe becomes merely a state of being.[16]

The fact that some of these MIB appear to be artificially constructed robots further adds to their enigma. I have no data from the time travelers concerning this observation. Our futuristic advisers didn't like to discuss the MIB. They are the futuristic "black sheep of the family."

Who are the Men in Black?

Many of the accounts of MIB, going back to biblical times, represent unexplainable phenomena by any scientific standard. I do not consider these reports hoaxes or delusions. That leaves us with four possible explanations.

The first and most common theory of the origin of MIB is as government agents. This can be given credence by those of us that have seen

---

16 M. Talbot, *Mysticism and the New Physics* (New York: Bantam Books, 1980).

or heard of the military's attempts to cover up UFO evidence. As part of this theory, some explain the Asian MIB as members of a secret Tibetan society who supposedly were brought by the CIA to the U.S. during the early 1950s. This most certainly doesn't explain the stories from ancient times of MIB, unless the Tibetans were time travelers.

One possible government agency to consider is the Air Force Special Activities Center (AFSAC), specifically the 1127th Field Activities Group. Alleged government collaborator William Moore states that this division is made up of shady characters and individuals who would think nothing of committing all sorts of crimes.

Another possible source is the Black Brotherhood. Involvement with malicious magic and other dark forces has been used to explain these men throughout history. The third possibility is that they could simply be the aliens that arrive in UFOs.

Lastly, these MIB could simply be the police force of our time travelers. This would explain many of the odd characteristics we have seen. MIB who are bumbling detectives of the future somehow seem more logical than the other paradigms. Of course, each possibility could be true in certain situations.

The otherworldly appearing MIB strongly suggest they are either hybrids or pure alien. The time travelers have definitely acknowledged these MIB as being other time travelers. Whenever they discuss the MIB it is almost with embarrassment, but as humorous as some of these MIB may appear, this is no laughing matter.

We can see that in certain instances these MIB (or were they just our regular time travelers?) have assisted in our growth. The Great Seal and Colonial flag episodes I reported reflect that principle. Most MIB incidences are quite negative, however, and have nothing to do with spiritual growth. It is no wonder the time travelers are embarrassed by the very existence of MIB.

When supernatural events are associated with MIB sightings, or fingerprints that cannot be traced (how could we identify fingerprints on someone who won't exist for at least 1,000 years?), or alien-like appearances are reported, I suspect these are futuristic cops. I do not doubt the other possibilities may exist also. Some MIB may very well work for the United States or other governments in some secret division.

Make no mistake, these MIB are real and many of them are from our future. They may appear incompetent and almost farcical, but they are always dangerous. It is quite typical of paranoid governments throughout history to require such repressive souls as part of the government's pact with the time travelers.

In ancient times and during the Middle Ages it was easy to prey on the black-magic mentality of the population in functioning as an MIB. Today the image of a government agent is more likely to be as a witness silencer. MIB have always been a part of our culture, and appear to also exist throughout our future.

Chapter 7

Unexplained phenomena revealed

The possibility of time travelers from our future visiting us and guiding both our biological and spiritual evolution is no more preposterous than having microorganisms assist in the biochemical processes within our bodies to preserve our health. Advances in science in the coming years, along with more direct contact from these chrononauts, will finally establish irrefutable evidence that beings from our future intervened on our history.

Evidence of visitations from time travelers is compelling. In some cases the data that follows were directly obtained from my patients during hypnotic regressions.

A nuclear explosion in 1908

A time traveler once informed a male patient that he had conducted experiments in our century in 1908 and 1913. No details were given other than it involved energy research. On June 30, 1908, an explosion more powerful than our heaviest hydrogen bombs occurred in Siberia. Trails of light were left by the trajectory of unidentified objects in the sky (UFOs). Following this explosion seismic shock waves and electromagnetic disturbances were felt all around the world. These effects are what we would expect to observe subsequent to a thermonuclear explosion.

At the time, mushroom clouds were observed by eyewitnesses. Some of these witnesses died a few years later from leukemia-like diseases, similar to those found in victims of the Hiroshima and Nagasaki atomic explosions. This occurred thirty-seven years before we had a workable nuclear bomb! An investigation of the site of this explosion by several Soviet scientific investigation teams revealed no meteorite debris, but they did find indisputable traces of radioactivity as late as 1963!

Many theories have been put forward to explain this event. The official Soviet paradigm fostered a collision between the Earth and a comet, but this theory fails to stand up because no such comet sighting was ever reported. Remember, Halley's Comet was due in 1910, so people would have been more alert to the sight of such a comet.

American scientists proposed a hypothesis focusing on a collision between a large quantity of anti-matter from space and that region of Siberia. This would theoretically cause the release of a tremendous amount of energy, as matter and anti-matter will annihilate each other upon contact.

But if this anti-matter entered our atmosphere from space, why didn't it create this explosion high above the Earth. Our atmosphere contains matter, and no viable theory explains how the anti-matter could have avoided an inevitable explosion prior to its reaching ground level.

To further complicate this picture, on the night of February 9, 1913 a second sighting occurred of luminous objects traveling in a group of four, followed by a group of three, then by a group of two. These objects were observed for more than three minutes by Professor C. A. Chant of the University of Toronto. The objects did not fall to the Earth as meteorites would have; their flight path appeared horizontal, and they traveled at a speed much slower than is recorded for meteorites.

The astronomer W. F. Denning of Canada noted that these objects originated from Canadian air space and flew over Bermuda, Brazil, and Africa, and eventually disappeared. Nobody ever noted their presence again. Only the lights from these objects, not the objects themselves, were seen. There were no rockets or artificial satellites being launched from the Earth in 1913.

Apparently what was alluded to by the time traveler's reference to 1908 and 1913 was an experiment that failed in 1908, but succeeded in 1913.

Spontaneous human combustion

One negative side effect on the magnetic forces around our planet from time traveling and experimentation by these chrononauts has been the rare case of spontaneous human combustion (SHC). When time travelers artificially create wormholes, they cause a tear in the fabric of space-time.

Although time travelers are not affected by this rip in space-time, in rare instances we humans are. In these instances the human body has ignited and burned without any known contact with an external source of fire.

We have reports of SHC dating back nearly 400 years. These reports show that an equal number of men and women are affected, in ages ranging from infancy to 114 years! Although some of these individuals combusted in the proximity of a source of fire, others have ignited while walking or driving in surroundings that lacked any external source of fire.

Modern science offers no sound physiological model for SHC, and cannot adequately explain how a human body could possibly self-ignite and burn with enough intensity to be reduced to ashes. It would require temperatures over 3,000°F to do this, yet clothing is sometimes discovered unscorched, a limb is found unaffected, and beds and chairs have been found intact, while the rest of the body is merely a pile of ashes.

The paradigm is alluded to by the time travelers. The numbers of electromagnetic fields surrounding our planet explain an alteration of the forces in our atmosphere that could create such a phenomenon. Let me reiterate, no matter how sophisticated the medical establishment or other conventional scientific community appears, contemporary science cannot offer any viable explanation for SHC. The time travelers have specifically stated that SHC is a consequence of their time traveling.

One might ask why this is still going on. We still hear reports today about such cases. The earlier chrononauts (about 1,000 years in our future) are responsible for this phenomenon by experimenting with forces they still don't quite understand. These well-meaning time travelers do make a lot of mistakes.

Why don't the more advanced time travelers (3,000 years in our future) simply use their advanced technology and correct this problem? I do not have an answer for that.

The spontaneous human combustion of Nicole Millet

This early report of SHC was observed by Jean Millet, an innkeeper in Rheims, France in 1725. On the night of February 19 the inn was full, as there was a big fair being held the following day. At approximately 2:00 in the morning Jean awoke and smelled smoke.

He rushed downstairs, alerting his guests by banging on the doors. When everyone arrived in the kitchen, the only thing ablaze was Nicole Millet, the innkeeper's wife, who was lying close to the fire. Nothing else was affected by this fire. All that remained of her body was part of her head, her lower limbs, and a few vertebrae.

Jean Millet was arrested for murder and tried in court. He was accused of pouring liquor over his wife's body and setting her on fire. One of the inn's guests was a physician named Claude-Nicolas Le Cat. The doctor was with the other guests when Nicole's body was discovered and he had examined it.

Le Cat testified on behalf of Jean Millet, stating that no human act could account for the total combustion of Nicole's body. Jean Millet initially was found guilty, but Le Cat's testimony eventually reversed this decision and Millet was released.[1]

A priest's SHC

In October 1776, a case was reported of an Italian priest, Don Gio Maria Bertholi, who caught fire during one of his preaching trips about the country. After arriving at his lodging one evening, he began to pray.

During one of his devotions, Don Bertholi cried out in severe agony. He was found on the floor surrounded by a light flame that receded as a physician, Dr. Battaglia, and others approached him. This flame soon vanished. Dr. Battaglia's examination revealed that the skin of the priest's right arm was almost entirely detached and hanging from the bone.

The skin was similarly affected from the shoulders to the thighs. Putrefaction had already begun on the right hand. Bertholi died on the fourth day. No diseases could be discovered by Dr. Battaglia, but the physician observed a "lambent flame" had attached itself to Bertholi's shirt, which was quickly reduced to ashes, although the cuffs remained untouched. The trousers were also unharmed, as was his head. Interestingly, Bertholi's cap was completely consumed, but there was no fire in Bertholi's room.[2]

The SHC of Mary Reeser

Mrs. Mary Reeser of St. Petersburg, Florida was discovered reduced to ashes in an apartment that was nearly completely intact. On July 1, 1951, Mrs. Reeser returned to her apartment after visiting her son, Dr. Richard Reeser.

The following morning a telegram arrived for Mrs. Reeser and was signed for by her landlady, Pansy M. Carpenter. When Mrs. Carpenter went to Mrs. Reeser's apartment to deliver this telegram, the doorknob was hot.

---

1 T. R. Beck and J. B. Beck, *Elements of Medical Jurisprudence* (Albany, NY: Little & Co., 1851), pp. 94–105.

2 Beck and Beck, op. cit., p. 198.

Two painters working across the street came in to open the door. When they did, a blast of hot air poured out of the apartment, but the only fire detected was a small flame on a wooden beam over a partition separating the kitchenette from the living room.

The fire department arrived and Assistant Fire Chief S. O. Griffith noted a charred area in the middle of the floor approximately four feet in diameter. Inside this area he found blackened chair springs, a charred liver attached to a piece of the spine, one foot with a black satin slipper on it, a shrunken skull, and a small pile of ashes.

Police, fire officials and arson experts were called in to investigate this case. Since little of the furniture, other than the chair and the adjoining end table, were badly damaged, these officials were at a loss to explain this occurrence.

The FBI was brought in and their investigation revealed that Mrs. Reeser's 175-pound body had been reduced to less than ten pounds, including the foot and shrunken head. No known chemical agents were detected that might have been involved in starting the fire. "Unusual and improbable" was the summation of this federal agency.

One observation in this case that is typical of other SHC phenomena is that the left foot was discovered intact. Mrs. Reeser had a habit of stretching out her left leg due to physical discomfort she suffered. Since this left foot was outside of the four-foot radius of incineration, it survived. This most unusual observation has been made in many other cases of this sort.

Experts ruled out an electrical fire as no blown-out fuses were found. Detective Cass Burgess of the St. Petersburg police stated on record:

> Our investigation has turned up nothing that could be singled out as proving, beyond a doubt, what actually happened. The case is still open. We are still as far from establishing any logical cause for the death as we were when we first entered Mrs. Reeser's apartment.

Police Chief J. R. Reichert commented:

> As far as logical explanations go, this is one of those things that just couldn't have happened, but it did. The case is not closed and may never be to the satisfaction of all concerned.

Dr. Krogman, an authority on burns, expressed his opinions:

> I have posed the problem to myself again and again of why Mrs. Reeser could have been so thoroughly destroyed, even to the bones, and yet leave nearby objects materially unaffected. I always end up rejecting it in theory but facing it in apparent fact.
>
> . . . the head is not left complete in ordinary burning cases. Certainly it does not shrivel or symmetrically reduce to a much smaller size. In presence of heat sufficient to destroy soft tissues, the skull would literally explode in many pieces. I . . . have never known any exception to this rule. Never have I seen a skull so shrunken or a body so completely consumed by heat.[3]

An SHC in a discotheque

Here we have a public sighting of the SHC of Maybelle Andrews. During the late 1950s, this nineteen-year-old girl was dancing with her boyfriend, Billy Clifford, in a London discotheque when she suddenly burst into flames. Although Clifford and others tried to save her, she died on the way to the hospital.

Clifford later was quoted as saying:

> I saw no one smoking on the dance floor. There were no candles on the tables and I did not see her dress catch fire from anything. I know it sounds incredible, but it appeared to me that the flames burst outward, as if they originated within her body.

His statements were corroborated by other witnesses. "Death by misadventure caused by a fire of unknown origin" was the official explanation.[4]

---

3 Michael Harrison, *Fire From Heaven: A Study of Spontaneous Human Combustion* (New York: Methuen, Inc., 1976), pp. 120–136.

4 Harrison, op. cit., pp. 93–94.

An SHC in a parked car

In October 1964, Mrs. Olga Worth Stephens was observed bursting into flames as she sat in a parked car in Dallas, Texas. The car was not damaged and contained nothing that could have started the fire, according to firefighters who investigated this case. Mrs. Stephens died as a result of her SHC.[5]

Infant SHC

In England two cases of SHC involving babies were reported during the early 1970s. The baby carriage holding seven-month-old Parvinder Kayr suddenly burst into flames in his parents' living room in 1973. No cause for this fire was ever given.

Six-month-old Lisa Tipton was found burned to death in a similar manner in her parents' home in Highfields, Staffordshire, on August 26, 1974. Again, no explanation for this fire was given.[6]

Some of the more silly attempts scientists have put forth to explain SHC are:

- Certain elements and compounds spontaneously burst into flames when exposed to air. This is true of phosphorus, for example, which is a component of the human body.

- Fats and oils, which the human body contains in abundance, are excellent fuels.

- Static electricity produces sparks that could, under certain conditions, set a body on fire.

- Haystacks and compost heaps can build up enough heat for spontaneous combustion.

- Intestinal gases are flammable.

Since many SHC cases involved people who drank a lot of alcohol and were near fireplaces, a study was conducted in which a rat was soaked in alcohol for a year, then set on fire. The skin blazed up and charred some outer layers of flesh, but the rat's internal tissues and

---

5   Ibid., p. 153.
6   Ibid., p. 261.

charred some outer layers of flesh, but the rat's internal tissues and organs were hardly affected. All of the above hypotheses and several others, ranging from lightning, internal atomic explosions, laser beams, microwave radiation, high-frequency sound, and geomagnetic flux, have been either tested or discussed, but none of these theories can explain how a person can burn to ashes, leaving the room and furnishings undamaged. To this day modern medicine refuses to classify this disorder.

The Nasca lines in Peru

The Nasca plateau in the Andes of southwestern Peru is forty miles long and six miles wide. The plateau is covered with small iron and silica stones coated with a black patina, forming complex designs that are impossible to detect while on the ground. These gigantic figures were discovered from the air in 1947, and German archaeologist Maria Reiche has studied them in detail.

The figures are made up of straight lines and large surfaces in trapezoidal form, giant spirals, and large-sized nonhuman figures, suggesting that the construction of these figures had to be monitored from the air by some type of craft.

From above, these lines appear to be like those we would observe at an airport, but they are not haphazardly constructed. From a central square measuring nine feet on a side are twenty-three straight lines approximately 600 feet long. One of these lines points to a spot in the sky corresponding to the solstice, and the other to the equinox. Is this some sort of astroport for time travelers?

One of my patients, an electrical engineer, had communication with chrononauts that supports this hypothesis. He was specifically told that the Nasca lines were their (the chrononauts') creation as a base for their crafts many thousands of years ago. The stones were moved using an anti-gravity device similar to that used in the construction of the Egyptian pyramids, as reported in Chapter 4.

The Nasca culture flourished from 300 B.C. to 400 A.D., but these lines were constructed somewhere between 12,000 B.C. and 3500 B.C. Peruvian legend names Manco Capac as the founder of the Nasca civilization. Manco Capac is not represented as an ordinary historical figure; it appears that his origin was from outside this civilization and without a specific location in time. This is because he was a time traveler!

Nasca line construction required technology far superior to that possessed by the local population. We see this same pattern in Stonehenge, the pyramids of Egypt, and the Mayan pyramids.

Interestingly enough, we can see the time traveler's influence on other aspects of this pre-Inca Peru civilization. Before any other ancient people knew about tourniquets, forceps, coca-based anesthetics, absorbent cotton, and gauze bandages for surgical incisions, Nasca inhabitants developed these forms of medical equipment. They also practiced bone transplants, cauterizations, excisions, and amputations, and portrayed these procedures on pre-Inca, and pre-Colombian pottery.

The use of hypnosis as an anesthetic prior to surgery can also be credited to these people. We find modern examples of this and other ancient secret sciences in the Collahu Aya, a Bolivian caste of medical priests. Although these priests will not discuss their practices, they bring with them as they travel throughout South America drugs that we cannot identify by chemical analysis.

The machining of platinum has been part of Peruvian culture since ancient times, yet the technology to do this was not developed by Europeans until 1730, and their techniques were *less* sophisticated than those of the Peruvian time traveler experiment! Even the Egyptians did not know about platinum.

Another reason we can't credit the Nasca culture of 300 B.C. to A.D. 400 as the builders of these lines was that they showed no other technological abilities. They built no pyramids or other megalithic structures.

Disappearances

The time travelers informed several of my patients that experiments in time travel with human subjects have been conducted. Some of them were successful in transporting these people into other periods of time, while others were dismal failures.

We must understand the humanness and susceptibility to error that are exhibited by these chrononauts. Some groups appear like "the gang that couldn't shoot straight," while others are highly efficient and nearly perfect in their duties.

The Philadelphia Experiment has been specifically mentioned several times as a time traveler project. During World War II on August 15, 1943, the *U.S.S. Eldridge* is reported to have disappeared, along with its crew of 181 sailors.

Dr. Nikola Tesla guided this project. Tesla himself was a time traveler protègè, according to the chrononauts. This project was of particular interest to certain less experienced time travelers in that it allowed them to map the Earth's magnetic field and more clearly facilitate hyperspace travel.

One main function of this experiment was to actually change both the past and future. Just prior to sunrise on August 15, 1943 the *Eldridge's* four massive generators, specially prepared for this experiment, were turned on to full power, and a strong electromagnetic field engulfed the ship.

Some reports stated a brilliant flash of light and piercing sound were sensed, and the ship disappeared. This ship apparently had been magnetically pulled through time and space. Their first stop was at Niagara Falls in the year 3543!

They then went back in time to:

- Great Salt Lake, Utah—2043
- Imperial Reservoir, California—2005
- Sebago Lake, Maine—1997
- Lake Mead, Nevada—1983. It was here that the ship stabilized and eighty-seven men were removed for research. Nineteen men

from 1983 came on board to accompany the remaining sailors
back to 1943. The ship arrived back at its original location on
August 16, 1943.

Four of these nineteen crew members added in 1983 were "timeliners." Were these specialists in time travel assigned by the military alone,
or working with our time travelers? I do not know the answer to that.

When the cleanup crew from 1983 completed their mission, they
boarded the *Eldridge* on August 18, 1943, and returned to 1983 at Mon-
tauk Point, Long Island (not Lake Mead), and became part of another
time travel research project. The timeliners remained in 1943.

Only twenty-one of the original 181 men survived. Twenty-seven
were literally embedded within the ship's structure, while 120 men were
removed in Nevada and New Mexico (a 1977 stop). Thirteen died of
radiation exposure, electrocution, and fright.

One rather interesting aspect of the Philadelphia Experiment that is
not often reported is what occurred in Philadelphia thirty-nine years
before that fateful day in 1943. Late in July of 1904 a ship called the
Mohican reported experiencing an unusual gray cloud that appeared to
attach itself to its hull and created unexplainable electrical effects, such
as uncontrollable spinning of compass needles and the magnetization of
metal objects on board.

A series of violent electrical storms were noted in Philadelphia at that
very time, along with strange lights moving around the city. Some
reports sited a strange ship in the Atlantic, not far from the location of
the *U.S.S. Eldridge* in 1943. Was this the *U.S.S. Eldridge* moving back in
time by thirty-nine years? That paradigm would most certainly be
compatible with the wishes of a time traveler-directed experiment, and
illustrates a tear in the fabric of space-time. As interesting as the Philadelphia Experiment was at the time, it must be classified as another
time traveler failed experiment.

The next cases I am about to present do attest to time travel experiments that had some measure of success. In each of these instances
the inhabitants were most probably sent to different time periods by
our chrononauts. These would indicate the earlier stages of time-
teleportation experiments by these time travelers.

In 1930 in the northern part of Canada, all of the inhabitants of the small Eskimo village of Angikuni disappeared. All the men, women and children were gone, but seven dogs tied to a tree were found dead of starvation. Eskimos do not leave a dog to die of hunger.

The Eskimos' guns were left behind, which is totally out of character. An Eskimo's gun is his most valuable asset. No explanation could be offered by local authorities.

A U.S. steamship, the *Iron Mountain*, disappeared in 1872. It was nearly 200 feet long and thirty feet wide. No trace of this ship or its fifty-five passengers and crew were ever found.

On November 10, 1939, during the Sino-Japanese War, 3,000 men commanded by Colonel Li Fu Sien disappeared completely. Their radio ceased transmitting, and all that was found were a few weapons. No Japanese records show the capture of an entire regiment at that time, and any mass desertion would have been known to their families.

On a forty-acre field near Gloucester, England, three children from the Vaughan family disappeared in the summer of 1906. A ten-year-old boy and his two sisters walked into this field and simply vanished. They were found four days later asleep in a ditch. Neither of them had any memories of what occurred.

The boy was interviewed forty years later and verified the above details. Although the official opinion of this case was a kidnapping, this would not explain the memory loss of the children. The Vaughan family was also quite poor, and it would not be logical for a kidnapper to take three children. The theory that this forty-acre field was part of a tear in the fabric in space-time, creating an entrance to and exit from the fifth dimension, certainly would explain this disappearance and the others I have cited.

On November 25, 1809, Benjamin Bathurst, the British Ambassador to the court of Francis I of Austria, vanished in the presence of his secretary and valet. He was never seen again. Although the British suspected Napoleon was somehow behind this mysterious disappearance, even French spies had no power to make a man vanish into thin air in front of two witnesses.

Cases of teleportation

Theoretical physics supports the contention that tears in the space-time continuum would allow for us to travel backward, forward, and sideways in time. This section will present cases mostly dealing with sideways teleportation. It must be remembered that in each case the fifth dimension is entered, and the principles of hyperspace apply.

The teleportation of a Spanish soldier

On October 25, 1593, a Spanish soldier suddenly appeared on the plaza in front of the palace in Mexico City. His uniform was unlike that of the other palace guards, and he carried a different type of gun.

When questioned later, this bewildered soldier stated that his orders were to guard the governor's palace in Manila! He insisted that he was from Manila, which is over 9,000 miles away and required at least several weeks travel time in the sixteenth century.

To prove his claim, he stated that the governor of Manila, Don Gomez Perez das Marinas, had been murdered the previous night. Mexico City authorities placed the soldier in prison. Two months later a ship arrived from the Philippines with news that the governor had indeed been murdered on the precise date claimed by this soldier! He was then released and sent back to his unit in Manila.

A 109-year trip back in time to Versailles

On August 10, 1901, two English schoolteachers, Anne Moberley and Eleanor Jourdain, were on vacation in Paris and touring the Palace of Versailles. Suddenly, they projected back in time to the Petit Trianon, the small château given by Louis XVI to Marie Antionette in 1792.

As they wandered through the pathways of this château, the teachers observed people dressed in eighteenth-century clothing. They even saw Marie Antionette painting on a canvas! What is interesting about this report is that by 1901 the Petit Trianon no longer existed. In addition, these two women described features of the landscape that matched those which actually existed in 1792, but not in 1901.

Cases involving clouds, gases, fogs, and mists

We have many reported cases of people being teleported from place to place in the presence of clouds, mists, fogs, and gases that seem to appear suddenly from nowhere, condense around a vehicle or person, and result in the sudden vanishing of the objects or people it encircles.

We observe unusual electromagnetic fields created, the appearance of water condensing onto the bodies of those who are teleported, unusual smells, rashes, headaches, bloodshot eyes, and tingly sensations. These coincide with symptoms of exposure to radiation.

Argentinian cases

Argentina appears to be the site of several fifth-dimensional openings or tears in the fabric of space-time. A businessman was driving south from Buenos Aires to Bahía Blanca in 1959 when suddenly a white cloud appeared out of nowhere and transported this man to a road unfamiliar to him.

As his car was not teleported with him, the businessman asked a truck driver where he was. It turns out that he was now in Salta, over 800 miles from Bahía Blanca. After contacting the local authorities, it was discovered that this man's car was exactly where he last recalled it to be, and the engine was still running.

Another case took place in 1968. In May of that year two cars containing family members on their way from a family gathering at Chascomus left Chascomus and were headed south toward Maipu. Traveling in one car were Dr. Gerardo Vidal and his wife Raffo of Buenos Aires.

The other couple reached Maipu with no problem, but the Vidal car never arrived. The Vidals called the other couple in Maipu two days later stating that they were unharmed but confused. A dense fog had appeared out of nowhere and engulfed their car. Their destination was an isolated country road in an unknown location.

The Vidals shortly discovered that they were in Mexico, over 4,000 miles away! To substantiate this fog, a man was admitted to a hospital in Maipu on the same night the Vidals were teleported; this man confirmed the presence of the fog. His experience with the fog was for just a few moments, but when it left, the watches of all those in the car had suddenly stopped.

British cases of teleportation

In October 1974, John Avis, his wife Sue, and their three children were returning home from a trip through a deserted countryside near London. A green fog encircled their car and sparks flew out of their car radio.

John pulled out the car radio wires and everyone soon felt a bump and a jolt as the car seemed to leave the ground and fall back to Earth suddenly. The mist was now gone and they soon arrived home, but two hours later than they were supposed to!

On February 9, 1988 a truck driver was walking along a road near Oswestry in Shropshire at 8:00 A.M. on a clear, sunny morning. He noticed an elderly woman with a dog walking alongside her.

Suddenly a yellow-white cloud emitting a noise like a motor appeared. The dog ran into this cloud and vanished. This rotating cloud, thirty feet in diameter, soon began to dissipate and vanished altogether. The dog lay on the ground panting heavily, soaking wet, and with bloodshot eyes. It recovered but died soon afterward of "natural causes."

The Bermuda triangle

Two small areas that have been the scenes of more disappearances than all the rest of the world put together are known as the "Bermuda Triangle" and the "Devil's Sea." One lies in the Atlantic off the east coast of the United States, the other in the Pacific, southeast of Japan. We will discuss the former.

The term "Bermuda Triangle" was coined by Vincent Gaddis, who also called it the "Triangle of Death." Gaddis was among the first to notice the incredible number of ships and aircraft disappearing in this relatively small area. Well over a hundred such disappearances have been recorded, with the loss of more than a thousand lives. Most of these mysteries have occurred since 1945, and the disappearances have been total. Not a single body nor a fragment of wreckage from the vanished crafts has ever been recovered. The infamous Sargasso Sea lies within the Bermuda Triangle.

In 1609 a ship called the *Sea Venture* was shipwrecked off the coast of Bermuda, on its way to Virginia bringing settlers to the New World. One of the longboats of the *Sea Venture* set out to the mainland of America to enlist aid. It was never seen again.

Five Spanish treasure ships encountered storms in this region and disappeared in 1750, and a search of the area turned up no evidence of any wreckage.

The number of lost ships and planes from this area east of Florida engendered even more interest from the U.S. government when Flight 19 vanished on December 5, 1945. Five Avenger torpedo bombers left Fort Lauderdale Naval Air Station on a training exercise that should have taken them over the Grand Bahama Island, then southwest back to their base.

Lieutenant Charles G. Carroll Taylor led this flight. He was an experienced aviator, but less than two hours after takeoff (2:10 P.M.) he sent the following radio message to the base: "Both my compasses are out. . . . I'm over land, but it's broken. I'm sure I'm in the Keys, but I don't know how far down and I don't know how to get to Fort Lauderdale." This message was interrupted by Lieutenant Robert Cox, who was flying over Fort Lauderdale on another exercise.

A transmission followed: "All planes close up tight . . . we will have to ditch unless landfall . . . when the first man gets down to ten gallons we will all land in the water together." A five-day search covering 250,000 square miles of ocean revealed no trace of Flight 19.

A 400-page naval inquiry record could not answer several questions. Why did both of Taylor's compasses fail shortly after they were checked out in the preflight inspection? Even though the northernmost Bahamas look much like the Florida Keys from the air, how did the airmen become convinced that the first leg of their flight had taken them so far south rather than east? The Navy could never explain how a planned two-hour training flight became a wandering, five-hour journey to nowhere. They conducted over 930 sorties over the area and found no evidence of a crash.[7]

British airliners, the *Star Ariel* and the *Star Tiger,* vanished in January 1949 while flying over the Sargasso Sea. All searches again turned up no physical evidence of these two planes. One interesting observation in reference to the disappearance of the *Star Ariel* was that both a British commercial plane and an American bomber reported sighting a strange light and a floating object that reflected the moonlight in the sea about 300 miles south of Bermuda. It was in the same area that *Star Ariel* had disappeared.

There is at least one incident on file of a pilot who survived the unexplained forces of the Bermuda triangle. Chuck Wakely, a chart plane pilot, in 1962 was returning from a solo flight from Nassau to Miami. He climbed to 8,000 feet, leveled off, and settled back for a routine run. Soon he noticed a faint glow on the wings of his plane.

As this glow increased in intensity it became impossible to read his instruments, so he used manual control of the plane. The wings glowed bluish green and looked fuzzy. Wakely had to release his controls, but was saved from disaster as the glow began to fade. When the glow finally died out the instruments began to work properly again and Wakely was able to make a safe landing at his destination.

Time travelers in ancient times

The time travelers claim that they have influenced all aspects of our development, including our religions. A detailed look at the Old Testament reveals some possible examples of time traveler intervention.

In Genesis we find: "And God said, Let us make man in our image."[8] The ancient Jews had one God. Where does the us fit into this? God could have just as easily said "my image." In another section of Genesis we find: "And it came to pass, when men began to multiply on the face

---

7   David Group, *The Evidence for the Bermuda Triangle* (Wellingborough, England: Aquarian Press, 1984).

8   Genesis 1:26.

of the earth, and daughters were born unto them, that the *sons* of God saw the daughters of men that they were fair; and they took them wives of all which they chose."[9]

Here we have a possible reference to the time travelers breeding with our ancient forefathers. The chrononauts have stated that they did breed with us. They repeatedly say that they engaged in all sorts of genetic experiments with our species.

Moses' construction of the Ark of the Covenant that was to contain the Ten Commandments is reported in Exodus. Specific directions were given to Moses as to how and where the staves and rings were to be fitted and which particular alloy the metals were to be made from. Moses was warned several times not to make errors with these detailed instructions.

A slipup did occur during the transporting of this ark. Uzzah grabbed hold of it when it shook and he fell dead on the spot, as if electrocuted. Some have attempted to reconstruct this Ark in modern times. The result is an electric generator producing several hundred volts of electricity.

We could even see how the time travelers could have used this as a primitive form of transmitter. The gold plates could create a condenser that was charged by the golden crown. When we add to this a magnet in the form of the cherubim on the mercy seat, the basics of a communication system are established. Sparks flashing around the Ark have been described. In this way our chrononauts could keep in communication with Moses when the former were on board their ship and/or Moses was at a distance away from them. These would have been earlier time travelers (about 1,000 years from our future).[10]

The Mahabharata

An ancient Indian epic, the *Mahabharata,* is at least 5,000 years old. It describes flying machines (Vimanas) that used quicksilver and a great propulsive wind to fly to great heights and travel upward, downward, backward, and forward. These flying machines had "an enormous ray

9 Ibid., 6:1–2.
10 Exodus 15:10.

which was as brilliant as the sun and made a noise like the thunder of a storm."

In the first book of this epic is an account quite similar to the story of Moses. A single woman named Kunti had a son by a "Sun god," but placed this child in a basket and took it to a river to avoid being disgraced. This child was retrieved by Adhirata, a Suta-caste man of excellent reputation, and brought up in his home.

In the eighth book of the *Mahabharata* we find out that Gurkha let loose a single projectile from a mighty Vimana that released white hot smoke a thousand times brighter than the Sun and completely destroyed a city. Here we have a nuclear explosion over 5,000 years ago.

The following passage from the *Mahabharata* is self-explanatory:

> It was as if the elements had been unleashed. The sun spun round. Scorched by the incandescent heat of the weapon, the world reeled in fever. Elephants were set on fire by the heat and ran to and fro in a frenzy to seek protection from the terrible violence. The water boiled, the animals died, the enemy was mown down and the raging of the blaze made the trees collapse in rows as in a forest fire. The elephants made a fearful trumpeting and sank dead to the ground over a vast area. Horses and war chariots were burnt up and the scene looked like the aftermath of a conflagration. Thousands of chariots were destroyed, then deep silence descended on the sea. The winds began to blow and the earth grew bright. It was a terrible sight to see. The corpses of the fallen were mutilated by the terrible heat so that they no longer looked like human beings. Never before have we seen such a ghastly weapon and never before have we heard of such a weapon.[11]

The time travelers did experiment with energy sources in ancient times and apparently made some miscalculations—I don't know why they would purposely try to wipe out a city by a nuclear attack.

---

11 P. Roy, *Mahabharata* (Calcutta: Bharata Press, 1978).

The Dead Sea Scrolls

Perhaps the answer to my last query can be explained by some citations from the Dead Sea Scrolls. In Cave 2 a translation was discovered of verses 25 through 32 of Genesis, Chapter 19:

25: The Lord (Elohim) instructed his Angels, both from the Morning and the Evening Star to assist Lot and his family to escape what was to befall the cities of Sodom and Gomorrah.

26. The two chosen ones instructed Lot and his family to drape themselves in white garments (fine linen) and run away from the cities with great haste.

27: Then a voice came from the darkening skies from on high and the other heavenly messengers, also from the Morning and Evening Star who rode in their chariots of fire say unto all of them below, "Make haste because the judgement of Almighty God is about to fall upon these evil cities. We are prepared to obey his Voice and point our fire spears toward the cities of sin and destroy them according to the Divine Will of the Father."

28: Then a white light as bright as the Sun blazed behind them and the Earth did shake with a might roar. The elements also did separate as the cities of sin were leveled to the ground. The air above the Earth was filled with destructive dust and every one including the animals did see life no more.

29: The smoke rose into the heavens and did cloak the ground with destruction.

30: Thus, the messengers from the stars did likewise accomplish their mission as their wheels returned to the skies where they rested with the others in their home which was high above the Earth.

31: She who was the wife of Lot, because of her disobedience, did turn around and gaze upon the destruction. She was turned into what appeared to be the salt of the land and the deadly destructive dust that clung over the Earth did indeed cause her life to cease.

32: The smoke and vapor from the cities rose higher and higher as the cities were laid to waste in the wilderness on the plains of Zoar that morning.

The salt that Lot's wife turned into may have been nuclear fallout vaporizing her body. I still don't have a logical reason for this nuclear explosion in ancient times.

A copper scroll found in Cave 3 depicts the time travelers' influence on our spiritual development. This focuses on Ezekiel's vision that is described in Chapter 1 of the Book of Ezekiel.

At the time of this description Ezekiel was part of a religious community called "NARU-KABARI TEL-ABIB," located near the river Chebar. Verses 29 through 38 describe a time traveler abduction with a happy ending:

29: The wheels did touch the Earth, the fire subsided, the door of the outer chamber opened and the silver pathway was lowered by the Angels.

30: His Angels beckoned to Ezekiel to come close and place his feet onto the silver pathway (ramp) and he proceeded to join together with the Angels.

31: They then sat and together broke bread and drank and had fellowship together.

32: Ezekiel was then shown the future as God so directed them. As they yet spoke, the silver pathway which came down was raised in the wheel

33: Ezekiel marveled at the wheel and the grandeur of seeing the Earth fall beneath his feet.

34: Among the marvels of the Earth below, Ezekiel saw the grandeur of the Sun, the Moon and the stars such as he never saw them before.

35: He wept aloud as the Angels of The Lord lifted their hands and their eyes and offered praise unto the Lord of Creation.

36: The wheel departed from the Earth high above that of the most powerful eagle.

37: Ezekiel saw and witnessed and understood the true meaning of Divine Fellowship between man and those who have come from afar to help the sons of men.

38: Sleep overcame Ezekiel and when he awoke, he found himself lying near the shore of the River Chebar. He witnessed and gazed upon the circle wherein the wheel had left its mark.[12]

The Book of Enoch

The time travelers are not publicity hounds. They work in the background, assisting humankind in our scientific, philosophical and spiritual growth. These futuristic time voyagers are not perfect. Their experiments sometimes fail and the people they put their faith and energy behind sometimes disappoint them.

Occasionally the time travelers are recorded in history and religious scriptures as gods. Mythology is full of references to these chrononauts. The apocryphal version of the Book of Enoch is not included in the official Old Testament. The oldest edition of this holy book was found in the Slavic countries around the tenth century A.D.

Enoch describes two time travelers as follows: "I received a visit from two men of very great height, such as I have never seen on Earth. And their faces shone like the sun, and their eyes were like two burning lamps. And fire shot forth from their lips. Their raiment looked like feathers. Their feet were purple, their eyes glistened more than the snow. They called me by my name."

Enoch later describes taking a trip and meeting the creator of the worlds. These time travelers explain how the Earth and the solar system were formed. For Enoch this trip took only a few days, but several centuries had elapsed on the Earth when he returned. Here we have an allusion to the theory of relativity, indicating that Enoch was traveling at close to the speed of light.

---

12 John M. Allegro, *Mystery of the Dead Sea Scrolls Revealed* (New York: Gramercy Pub. Co., 1982).

The Five Kingdom experiment

One of many experiments with the development of our species was in accelerating our technology in building construction. A reference was made by one of my patients to the Five Kingdoms in the Middle East. I had never heard of this civilization before.

In the Hadhramaut desert ancient skyscrapers have been discovered that belonged to the lost civilization. Arabia Felix arose during the second century B.C. and existed until about the first century A.D., but there are prehistoric sites dating back 75,000 years.

Arabia Felix was made up of five kingdoms: Saba, Quataban, Habhramaut, Ma'in, and Hausan. The Mukkaribs, magician-priests under the guidance of time travelers, governed these kingdoms. By 1500 B.C. a Semitic culture flourished, specializing in the export of incense, a commodity in great demand by the ancient world. Remember the frankincense and myrrh given to the baby Jesus by the three Wise Men?

These civilizations built large canals, substantial dams, and nine-story skyscrapers. It required the anti-gravity techniques of the time travelers to complete these buildings.

The technology exhibited by the structures in Arabia Felix could not be duplicated by its successive conquerors, Ethiopians, Persians, and Arabs.

Some Arab texts describe a twenty-story skyscraper built during the first century A.D. of granite, porphyry, and marble. This structure has not been found, however.

Another mystery about the Arabia Felix civilization is that they would have had to master mathematics to build their canals and dams. Yet no trace of the mathematics of Arabia Felix has survived, although we do have intimate knowledge of Babylonian mathematics. There is no current trace of this lost civilization—as the time travelers admitted, it was one of their many failed experiments. They took their secrets with them when they abandoned Arabia Felix.

Reincarnation

It really isn't logical for primitive and savage humankind to express an interest in reincarnation, yet we find time and time again an obsession with the idea of immortality of the soul. Slaves willingly allowed themselves to be killed so they could join their masters in a future life.

The Pyramid texts in Egypt contain an inscription that says, "Thou art he who directs the sun ship of millions of years."[13] Where does ancient man get the concept of millions of years? One sign of eternity and external life in the ancient world was the winged Sun and a soaring falcon, still seen on the doors to the temples at Idfu in Egypt. Only Egypt has so many winged symbols of the gods depicted in their art. Perhaps the time travelers are responsible for this concept of reincarnation.

One way to find answers to these questions would be to review the scrolls from the ancient libraries. Unfortunately we have lost over ninety-five percent of these works of ancient wisdom. The 500,000 volumes belonging to Ptolemy Soter in Alexandria, Egypt, were partly destroyed by the Romans during Caesar's reign. The rest were stupidly burned by Caliph Omar in the seventh century A.D.

The libraries of the temple at Jerusalem, Pergamon (200,000 volumes), Ephesus (destroyed by the Apostle Paul), China (in 214 B.C. Emperor Chi-Huang ordered a massive destruction of scrolls) and an unknown number of other wanton burnings were carried out by narrow-minded autocrats.

Lascaux, France, is the location of caves that contain prehistoric paintings completed about 20,000 years ago. We don't know why these cave walls were so decorated, nor how light was provided to do this beautiful art. Savage Stone Age cavemen could not have exhibited such artistic talent. If they could do these murals, why not build better accommodations, such as huts?

On the west coast of Borneo, in the Subis Mountains, a network of caves was discovered that had been hollowed out on a massive scale. How was this accomplished? Fabrics of great delicacy and fineness were

---

13 E. A. W. Budge, *The Book of the Dead* (London: Longman & Co., 1895).

also discovered in these hidden caves. Time traveler technological influence is evident in these examples.

Easter Island

Imagine that you are a European sailor arriving on Easter Island at the beginning of the eighteenth century. Hundreds of colossal statues lie scattered all over this little island 2,350 miles from the coast of Chile.

How could the island inhabitants of a distant past possibly have carved these steel-hard volcanic rocks, some weighing as much as fifty tons? Some of these figures had stone hats that weighed more than ten tons each, and originated at a different site from that of the bodies. No primitive technology could have hoisted these ten-ton structures high enough to place them on the bodies of the stone carvings.

We have seen how anti-gravity crafts were used by the time travelers in ancient Egypt to build the pyramids at Giza and also at Stonehenge in England. These same devices were undoubtedly used here. There simply wasn't enough manpower for the inhabitants of Easter Island to have created these stone carvings.

The island dwellers referred to their land as the "Land of the Bird Men," and still do today. Legends abound of flying men (time travelers) from ancient times. Without the local stone resources to build these statues and the technology to move massive weights of stone from place to place on this island, we must look for another explanation. Based on what the time travelers have stated concerning their interaction with our species since ancient times, my vote is with the chrononauts.

We can see a common pattern of moving large tonnages of stones in ancient times to build structures that had nothing to do with providing basic life services for the people. In Egypt the obelisk material came from Aswan, and the stone blocks of Stonehenge originated from distant quarries in southwest Wales and Marlburough, and was transported by some unknown means. I don't think ancient man was that masochistic. The time travelers' anti-gravity crafts made their work a whole lot easier.

Flying hay

In Wrexham, England, on a calm summer day in the late nineteenth century, hay was observed flying under its own power. This most unusual event took place at 2:00 P.M. on a July day.

Approximately 1,000 pounds of hay sailed above the Welsh town of Wrexham through the sky. What was even more interesting was that the hay moved in a northerly direction, which was against the wind. The hay traveled a distance of about five miles before it fell back to Earth.

Unexplained events in India

A large meteorite covered with ice crashed down in Dhurmsalla, India, on July 28, 1860. This event was documented by the British Deputy Commissioner at the time. We certainly don't expect to see ice-covered meteorites, since most of them are white-hot from entering our atmosphere and plunging to Earth.

Lights in the sky were observed the following evening. They couldn't have been from planes, as this occurred over forty years before planes were invented. They could very well have been our time travelers.

Other unusual events around this time included a report of a shower of live fish at Bonares, a long period of darkness during daylight hours, and a red blood-like substance that fell from the sky at Farrukhabad.

In 1861 an earthquake was reported in Singapore. Following this there were three days of torrential rain. In the pools of water formed by this rain, fish were observed swimming. Dead fish were discovered on the ground when these pools dried up.

One explanation for the fish was that they came from a river that overflowed. A reporter who documented this phenomenon also found fish in his courtyard, but his home had a high wall that kept the water out. The fish *must* have come from the sky.

The Oregon vortex

There is a place in Sardine Creek, Oregon, called the "Oregon Vortex." On this spot, approximately 165 feet across, the force of gravity appears intensified as you move toward its center. Certain instruments, such as a photographer's light meter and compasses, simply go haywire in this area.

An abandoned hut that has slipped downhill and currently lies at a slight angle toward the center of this circle produces a strange sense of unbalance for those who enter it. For instance, a ball dangling from a beam in the ceiling of the hut seems to incline toward the center of the vortex. Objective observations made from the perspective of beyond this unusual region confirm this.

Visitors feel pulled toward the center of the circle, and seem compelled to lean backward at an angle. Cigarette smoke in the vortex spirals upward in a strange manner, and a handful of confetti whirls around as if caught in a twister.

We know that waves of space-time are not fixed, but roll across the universe in a definite rhythm. Certain spots could be freakish and unpredictable. Add to this the possibility of a tear in the fabric of space-time and the creation of fifth-dimension gateways and we can see how such strange phenomena could occur. The time travelers have stated that some of their early experiments resulted in permanent rips in space-time. Was this one of them?

Chapter 8

Time traveler experiments

It should not come as a great surprise that many of the unexplained phenomena and anomalies that have stumped our greatest minds were the results of time traveler experiments. These chrononauts have molded our growth as a species as far back as sixty-five million years ago!

The earlier chrononauts (approximately 1,000 years from our future) conducted many experiments that simply failed. Their failure can be seen in a lack of spiritual growth in our civilization today, to say nothing of technological failures.

We have seen nuclear explosions in ancient times, and failed civilizations one after another. The later time travelers (2,000 to 3,000 years in our future) don't appear to make these mistakes. I still do not know why these more advanced time travelers don't simply repair the errors of their predecessors. Only time will answer that question.

Dinosaur extinction

We cannot explain with absolute certainty the disappearance of the dinosaurs approximately sixty-five million years ago. Many theories have been proposed, from diseases to meteorites.

Other animals fed on dinosaur eggs, but this was not the case with ichthyosaurs that laid their eggs in the oceans, well out of the reach of predators.

The grasses changed and the new tougher textured ones were unsuitable for the herbivores, but large numbers of other grasses and other vegetation survived that would have easily met their needs. Consider the giant tortoises of the Galápagos Islands that have been around since the dinosaurs. They survived.

It is true that after several hundred million years nature simply eliminates a species. However, cockroaches and crabs have remained viable after several hundred million years.

We have all heard of the infamous meteorite hitting the Earth at the Yucatan village of Chicxulub Puerto sixty-five million years ago, resulting in a great change in our climate, but that would not explain why the dinosaurs living in the ocean died also.

The time travelers have reported that they purposely extinguished the dinosaurs to speed up the evolution of humankind, and subsequently themselves. Left to their own devices, the dinosaurs would have lived another twenty million or more years. To bring about their end, the time travelers arranged for a supernova that produced a radiation shower killing these large beasts without destroying the other species.

Is it so far-fetched to conceive of the idea that our future representatives, ranging from 1,000 to 3,000 years ahead in time, could master astrophysics to the extent that they bring this phenomenon about? Eminent Russian astrophysicist I. S. Chklovski studied synchrotron radiation and demonstrated that rapid and violent events can be produced at the center of galaxies and in space itself.

Chklovski proposes that a supernova star at five or ten parsecs (one parsec equals 3.26 light years) from Earth would significantly increase the density of cosmic radiation. English radio astronomer Hanbury Brown detected traces of a supernova that took place about fifty thousand years ago at approximately forty parsecs from our solar system.

Radiation bombardments from exploding stars have been observed by K. D. Terry of the University of Kansas and W. H. Tucker of Rice University in Texas. The intensity of the Earth's magnetic field protects us from these bombardments. A thinner magnetic field (produced by the time travelers) could have resulted in mutations that could easily have killed off the dinosaurs and speeded up the evolution of mammals into modern humans.

Two of my patients, who did not know each other, have independently stated that the time travelers confirmed this hypothesis—they genetically altered the DNA of both the dinosaurs and mammals to allow us to evolve as we did. Time travelers have been genetically altering mammals for at least sixty-five million years.

These time travelers had a premeditated plan to initiate a supernova star, killing off the dinosaurs and genetically making it possible for humankind to arise with the intelligence we possess. This hypothesis is not so far-fetched. Consider the fact that the greatest source of energy we have is the H-bomb. This device converts hydrogen to helium. There is plenty of hydrogen in our Sun, or any other Sun, with which to create such a star explosion.

Think for a moment of the fact that we use only from one to ten percent (a very generous estimate) of our brain. If time travelers merely double this use, what limits would they have in brain power and technological developments?

One possible mechanism to accomplish the dual purpose of eliminating the dinosaurs and speeding up our evolution could involve the production of very short wavelength or particle radiation. This transmission would need to be modulated in order to transfer the DNA equivalent to image transfer by a television channel. Very short gamma-ray band waves could work with this paradigm.

There is absolutely nothing in science today that makes the paradigms I presented impossible, or even unlikely. Killing off the dinosaurs with massive radiation and genetically altering surviving mammals with smaller and more selective radiation doses is a distinct possibility.

Time traveler protégés

The time travelers have stated that they trained many inhabitants of our planet in science, philosophy and spiritual growth techniques—specifically mentioned were Benjamin Franklin, Saint-Germain, and Joseph Priestly. Another interesting name that surfaced was Sir Henry Cavendish, who apparently was tutored by the time travelers throughout most of his life. He was a time traveler protégé.

The man who called himself Sir Henry Cavendish was reportedly born October 10, 1731, in Nice, France. He died in Clapham, England on February 24, 1810, having lived a life of luxury, characterized by philanthropy. To this day nobody knows where he obtained his wealth, as he was born into a poor family.

Throughout his life Cavendish made many generous contributions to charities of all kinds. He was reputed to be one of the greatest scientists of his time, although he never earned a degree. Cavendish was admitted to the Royal Academy of Sciences in 1760 at the age of twenty-nine. He was the youngest man to achieve such a feat, and this honor was bestowed on a man who never published a scientific article, and had no scientific degree! Although Cavendish did attend Cambridge University, he never graduated.

Sir Henry pursued a secret life for approximately thirty years. The details of that time in his life are unknown. He was definitely an "odd chap." Cavendish was extremely wealthy by the time he died. He had been a principal stockholder in the Bank of England, but had not worked a day in his life. Remember, this same man gave away large sums of money to charity.

This time traveler's protégé left no portrait of himself, kept hidden the many projects he worked on in his various laboratories, used alchemy symbols to designate metals and planets, and was centuries ahead of his time. For example, Cavendish calculated the deviation of light rays by the Sun's mass and arrived at a number very close to Einstein's figure. In addition, he isolated rare gases from the air, and accurately computed the mass of our planet.

On May 27, 1775, Cavendish invited seven renowned scientists to his modest lab and demonstrated electricity, long before Galvani and Volta did. Scientists of his era knew nothing of electrons, yet Cavendish discussed electricity in terms of a fluid and measured electric voltage.

Cavendish studied alchemy and used its symbols throughout his life. He benefited from the secret knowledge of the time travelers who guided him every step of the way. Cavendish's work brought to the surface such concepts as relativity, electricity, and atomic energy. Unfortunately for science, the main components of Cavendish's scientific work were not published until 1921, 111 years after his death.

Other protégés of the time travelers included Roger Boscovitch, who in 1756 published treatises depicting time travel, bilocation, parallel universes, antigravitation, quantum theory, and relativity. English mathematician Cayley invented the airplane in 1800, and submitted to the Royal Society of Science in England his mathematical studies describing a motor strong enough to propel a plane through the air.

One of the emissaries of the time travelers in England was an organization called the Invisible College. This group included such eminent scientists as Sir Christopher Wren (1632–1723), Robert Boyle (1627–1691), John Wilkins (1614–1672), Thomas Sidemham (1624–1689), and Isaac Newton (1642–1727).

The organization's purpose was to reveal a certain number of the universe's secrets to the world. It received a charter in the name of the Royal Society of Science from King Charles II of England in 1662. These gentlemen were all Masons.

The Royal Society of Science discriminated between those secrets it decided were too dangerous to reveal to the world versus those it felt the planet could handle. The time travelers directed this group, along with other scientific societies such as the French Academy of Science, the New York Academy of Science, and many others.

Here is a good example of futuristic knowledge that preceded its practical application. Roger Boscovitch, in the eighteenth century, as did Cavendish, encouraged the exploitation of rubber. This material was available only in small quantities in Europe at that time.

The concept of a manmade satellite projected into space by a cannon can be traced back to Newton. Jules Verne read about it in the annals of the Ecole Polytechnique and used the concept as the basis of his *From Earth to the Moon.*

The Medieval experiment

The jury is out about whether or not the time traveler's Medieval experiment worked. I have several accounts in my files about the time travelers' role in Medieval times. We can look to the alchemists and mystics of the Middle Ages as examples of the influence of the time travelers.

We hear stories such as a strange series of fires during the great plague in London that only consumed those homes that were contaminated. This fortuitous event kept the epidemic from spreading to the entire English population. No doubt time travelers were behind this.

Instead of looking at the Middle Ages as a period of darkness, let us analyze more objectively its accomplishments. The term *demon* as used in the Middle Ages referred, in the Socratic sense, to a being that debated with you and supplied ideas. Demons were not the evil creatures Hollywood would lead us to believe.

These demon time travelers stimulated citizens of the Middle Ages to learn the secrets of the universe through experimentation. Some Medieval writers conjectured that the origin of these demons was from parallel universes, although they never used that precise expression.

The astronomer Kepler described himself being transported to the moon by a benevolent demon who assisted him with his research. Time travelers were then described as creatures with "garments of light" who met with rabbis discussing the Kabbala, the powers of God, and the theory of time travel.

These chrononauts appeared to saints and have been described since before the time of Christ. They possess three characteristics: a double face, a luminous garment, and the crown of the king of glory (a luminous halo surrounding the time traveler). Portraits of saints often depict this image, and we have explored the role of time travelers as guardian angels in Chapter 5.

The "double face" is most likely a reference to space helmets, while the "luminous garment" could have described an aura of luminous radiation or fluorescence surrounding their jumpsuits. The Freemasons called themselves "Sons of Light" to allude to this luminous quality. It must be remembered that the Masons were often led and organized by actual time travelers.

If there is one common source of time travelers throughout the Middle Ages it is through the Freemasons. Some trace the Masons back to ancient Egyptian and Hermetic disciplines. Unfortunately, undisputed documents demonstrate that Masonic lodges date back to Scotland in 1599, but nothing before that.

English freemasonry reportedly began with the discovery of a secret tomb containing a perpetual lamp. These perpetual lamps functioned without oil or any other flammable substance. We find references to these time traveler inventions in Jewish, Islamic, and Rosicrucian writings. It was forbidden to touch the lamps; to do so was to cause an explosion capable of leveling an entire town. Is this not the effect we would expect from matter coming into contact with anti-matter from a parallel universe?

One of the best examples of a Medieval time traveler protégé was Roger Bacon. Bacon was born in 1214 and became a monk of the order of St. Francis. He taught at Oxford University, and his works prophesied airplanes, microscopes, steam engines, and telescopes.

Since no one was allowed to question the works of Aristotle and others, Bacon promoted the concept that scientists should study mathematics and perform experiments to discover the truth. Bacon was considered insane and imprisoned for fourteen years. He died in 1294, and the time travelers consider their work with him a failed experiment.

In 1912 a rare-book specialist named Wilfrid Voynich purchased a manuscript at the Mondragone Jesuit school in Frascati, Italy. The manuscript was allegedly written by Roger Bacon, and presented to Emperor Rudolph II in 1585 by the alchemist and magician John Dee, who was unable to decipher it.

Voynich took this manuscript to the United States, where its most brilliant decoders could not unravel its secrets. Finally Professor William Romaine Newbold partially decoded this work. Roger Bacon has apparently established that the Andromeda nebula was a galaxy; he understood chromosomes and their function and constructed a microscope and telescope.

Since the coding system used in this manuscript constantly changed, Newbold could not complete his work. He died in 1926. I believe Bacon could not have made these discoveries without the assistance of the time travelers. His manuscript was written in an artificial language (the first use of such languages dates from the seventeenth century, or 400 years ahead of Bacon's time).

The Voynich manuscript, as it has been named, appears to make sense and is not considered to be a hoax. It is written in the language of the time travelers, and contains secrets we are not yet supposed to know.

Many mysterious disappearances and returns were reported during the Middle Ages. A number of people claimed to have visited a country called Matagonie, according to Archbishop Agobard of Lyons (779–840). Their trips were by way of airships, and very little time had elapsed during the trip compared to their world when they returned.

The Egyptian experiment

Dating back to at least 10,500 B.C., time travelers representing various periods in our future visited the ancient Egyptians and presented varying levels of technology and spirituality to them. The time travelers failed in their attempts to raise spiritual growth levels among these ancients.

The dominant religion of the major cultures throughout the ancient world (Egypt, India, China, Greece, Rome, etc.) was the Mystery Schools. This sect took a paranoid stance toward educating the masses about the secrets of the universe—hence the term *Mystery Schools.*

Only initiates (*catechumen*) were allowed the privilege of this knowledge, as they required the service of a guide (*hierophant*) to protect them in this pursuit. My clinical work conducting over 33,000 past life regressions on more than 11,000 individual patients since 1974 has established that most of these ancient Egyptians reincarnated in ancient Greece and Rome and continued making the same karmic errors over and over again. In other words, as a result of time traveler intervention, these ancients simply did not grow spiritually.

Ancient Egypt was an authoritarian theocracy characterized by high priests who murdered their pharaohs (King Tut, for example) when the ruler would not carry out these priests' wishes. Poison was the most common method of eliminating the pharaohs.

The principle of slavery practiced by the Egyptians hardly qualifies as spirituality. Theirs was a militaristic lifestyle, characterized by arrogance and stubbornness. Although enlightenment was the chief purpose of their religion, it failed miserably, as history has demonstrated.

The time travelers' influence on these ancients was demonstrated in a case I presented in my first book, *Past Lives—Future Lives.* The chapter titled "Hubert Meets Aliens in Egypt" presented a past life of a man involved in the construction of the Great Pyramid of Giza:

Dr. G.—What exactly does your position involve?

Hubert—I cut slots into the stones so that they will fit into the pyramid.

Dr. G.—Do you like your job?

Hubert—I'm very skillful at my work, but they won't listen to my ideas about moving the stones.

Dr. G.—Who are they?

Hubert—The directors.

Dr. G.—Can you describe these directors?

Hubert—They are very tall, around seven or eight feet tall. They have large heads and long fingers.

Dr. G.—How do the directors communicate with you?

Hubert—They don't talk at all. They seem to send out some sort of thought signals which compels me to obey them. I, I don't feel that I can resist them at all.

When I inquired about the techniques used to build this structure, Hubert answered as follows:

Hubert—They have special ropes. I've never seen rope like it before. It is very strong and doesn't seem to break. They also have a cranelike apparatus that runs on a battery of some sort.[1]

We have already seen from other past life regressions taking place at this time the presence of other time travelers (I cannot be sure Hubert's directors were time travelers; they may have been somewhat primitive extraterrestrials) who used anti-gravity vehicles to aid in the construction of this pyramid. Too many chefs were at work.

From a technological perspective, the time travelers were successful in building the pyramids and the Sphinx, but this technology was short lived and disappeared after they left. The three pyramids built at Giza were constructed during Egypt's early pyramid-construction phase. In addition, the hieroglyphics in these structures, known as the *Pyramid Texts* and forming the basis of the *Egyptian Book of the Dead,* were unsurpassed in artistic quality and degenerated considerably in future generations.

For only 100 years technologically superior pyramids were built and artistically beautiful hieroglyphics were produced. There were no predecessors to either of these achievements (something that automatically suggests an advanced influence to these ancients), and subsequent attempts to duplicate this technology and art failed miserably.

Returning for a moment to the pyramid construction at Giza, my regressions illustrate the presence of anti-gravity vehicles that assisted in

---

1   Goldberg, *Past Lives* (1988) pp. 90–91.

moving and placing the large stones during certain, but not all, phases of the construction of these pyramids.

The time travelers report that they purposely kept away from others who were working on these structures, as with Hubert's directions. However, the anti-gravity crafts used by the time travelers were most interesting in design and function, as we have seen.

A decoding of the true significance of the pyramids at Giza will eventually occur, according to the chrononauts. For now, let me relate what little information I have pieced together. The mathematical functions coded within the Great Pyramid create an invisible timepiece of higher evolutionary movements as a clock placed on the face of the Great Pyramid. These mathematics tell us the angle of the slope of the outside of the Great Pyramid is 51°51'14.3". The altitude of the Great Pyramid is to the length of one side of the base as 1 is to ½π (Pi). The length of the Ante-Chamber multiplied by 100 is 11,626.02 pyramid inches. Using this figure as the diameter of a circle or the altitude of the pyramid as the radius of a circle, the circle is equal in area to a square whose side is 10,303.30 Pyramid inches in length, thus squaring the circle.

The squaring of the circle is one of the greatest mathematical calculations known in the calculus of the ancient Egyptian priest-scientists who were concerned with the greater solar movement, for it allowed them to use the astrophysical tables given by the time travelers that were placed in the Pyramid.

The solution is the understanding of how terrestrial and solar movement are tied together in the greater "Precession of the Equinoxes"—the 26,000-year cycle which connects with our embryonic cycles of time as calculated by the time travelers. This precession of the equinoxes is the length of time required for our solar system to make one complete revolution around the Pleiades, our greater parent Sun, which calculates to a period of 25,827.5 years.

The Great Pyramid contains the distance from the Earth to the Sun—the solar energy form of local creation, but the relationship to the cradle and throne of our consciousness cycle of creation is given in four codes of the physical pyramid:

- Each of the two base diagonals of the Great Pyramid taken together equals 25,827.5, the Precession of the Equinoxes, at the rate of an inch per year.

- The width of the Grand Gallery of the Great Pyramid times π (3.14159) equals 25,827.5, the Precession of the Equinoxes.

- The altitude of the Great Pyramid lying above the floor-plane of the King's Chamber times π (Pi) equals 25,827.5, the Precession of the Equinoxes.

- The King's Chamber is situated on the fiftieth plane of masonry in the Great Pyramid. The outside surface perimeter at this level in original Pyramid inches equals 25,827.5, the length of the Precession of the Equinoxes.

The Great Pyramid is a geophysical computer showing the relationship of our local universe within the geophysical foundations of the Earth's biophysical, geophysical, and astrophysical meridians. This structure is a model for the light continuum of the many universes connected with our Earth.

The *Pyramid Texts* speaks of the builders of the Pyramid, the Nine, who programmed in the direction of Orion: "In your name of Dweller in Orion, with a season in the sky and a season on earth. O Osiris, turn your face and look on this King, for your seed which issued from you is effective." Another text gives forth the sacred message: "The sky conceiveth thee together with Orion, the dawn beareth thee together with Orion. Live the one who liveth at the order of the gods and so will thou live."

These two fragments from the ancient Egyptian scriptures show the direct relationship between the Pyramid and Orion through the body of death and resurrection of the Ascended Master Osiris. And as we look deeper at the meaning of the Pyramid, we are to understand how it gives the model for human consciousness resurrection.

The star shafts in the Great Pyramid are intended as the introductory ways of consciousness preparation, whereby not only Osiris' soul but the souls of all those who have been initiated into the Pyramid might actually ascend to the higher planes to join God.

To this end, the Pyramid can be understood as the model for conscious exodus from one three-dimensional time-set within the Earth's magnetic fields into a multi-dimensional evolution, with ascension as its ultimate goal

Robert Bauval's work shows just how accurate the three pyramids of Giza reflect the Orion Belt of planets:

> They're slanted along a diagonal in a south-westerly direction relative to the axis of the Milky Way and the pyramids are slanted along a diagonal in a south-westerly direction relative to the axis of the Nile. If you look carefully on a clear night you'll also see that the smallest of the three stars, the one at the top which the Arabs call Mintaka, is slightly offset to the east of the principal diagonal formed by the other two. This pattern is mimicked on the ground where we see that the Pyramid of Menkaure is offset by exactly the right amount to the east of the principal diagonal formed by the Pyramid of Khafre (which represents the middle star, Al Nilam) and the Great Pyramid, which represents Al Nitak. It's really quite obvious that all these monuments were laid out according to a unified site plan that was modeled with extraordinary precision on those three stars . . . What they did at Giza was to build Orion's Belt on the ground.[2]

I find it hard to believe that the ancient Egyptians were able to move 2.3 million limestone blocks, averaging two and a half tons each, and that they somehow carried these massive stones in ships from a site 400 miles down the Nile to lever them together with hairline precision, displaying an accuracy of engineering that couldn't be duplicated today. No, I much prefer the explanation of an advanced human race with anti-gravity flying cars.

The time travelers stated that there are certain energy grids on our planet that become like large wormholes, permitting these chrononauts to enter the fifth dimension and travel back in time. These electromagnetic grid patterns of star alignment with certain points on the Earth are

---

2   R. Bauval and A. Gilbert, *The Orion Mystery* (London: William Heineman, 1994).

vortex points of a magnetic field that become "time tunnels" when they touch down at specific surface points.

Some examples of these time tunnels are: Stonehenge, the Pyramids of Giza, the Mayan pyramids, Mount Shasta in California, certain regions of the Himalayas, some locations in the Peruvian mountains, and many areas in the deserts throughout the world. In the United States, there are several locations in New Mexico and Nevada that are very popular with chrononauts.

In the example of the Great Pyramid, this structure is activated to produce a wormhole time tunnel by being coordinated with other such grids on this planet. When the secrets of this great structure and the Sphinx are revealed, we will be able to enter the fifth dimension and travel back or forward in time.

This magnetic vortex effect helps to explain Old Testament stories such as the parting of the Red Sea by Moses, or the raising of the dead by Jesus in the New Testament. In Moses' case, the Old Testament states: "Moses was instructed in all the wisdom of Egypt."[3]

Ley lines

In the 1920s Alfred Watkins, a businessman and amateur archeologist, observed that whole areas of the English countryside are criss-crossed with straight lines, indicating ancient tracks that join hilltops, churches, and prehistoric monuments. He called these lines "leys." Could these ley lines be the energy grids the time travelers alluded to?

Hundreds of people have mapped these ley lines all over England. Many sites from ancient times align along these ley lines. For example, there is a ley line connecting Salisbury to Stonehenge. The theory is that these ancient monuments might serve as condensers of electrical forces. They might also unite spiritual forces.

Consider the fact that one of these ley lines runs through a great stone circle at Glastonbury, the site of the legends of King Arthur and

---

3   Acts 7:22.

early Christianity.[4] We can hypothesize that these ley lines are somehow involved in creating wormholes for our time travelers.

Ley lines have been reported in primitive magic systems, such as the *Mana* of the Polynesian Islands. These lines appear to be located along channels of geophysical power. Ancient people may have sensed this force, or been instructed by the time travelers to use these sites, and constructed their monuments where the energy was the strongest. A *node* is an intersection of leys, and could very well be the wormhole time machine used by the chrononauts.

We must remember that the leys were manmade, according to Watkins, and these tracks, he deduced, were initially laid down between 4,000 and 2,000 B.C. Even early Christian churches were built on leys. These leys linked prehistoric barrows, dolmens, stone circles, pagan altars, and medieval churches also.

In the 1850s William Pidgeon found analogous lines in America connecting Indian burial grounds. The German regional planner Dr. Josef Heinsch noted "holy hills" in his native land. So did a fellow countryman named Wilhelm Teudt, who labeled his find as "holy lines."

The Nasca lines in Peru and western Bolivia's *takiis,* or "straight lines of holy places," are other examples of leys. We find unusual events in or near these lines. For example, there have been many UFO sightings around Stonehenge. In August 1936 Stephen Jenkins viewed a group of medieval warriors on the Cornish coast near where King Arthur is supposed to have died. The scene vanished shortly, but reappeared and disappeared on this same spot thirty-eight years later!

Another unexplained phenomenon took place in Chanctonbury Ring, an ancient earthwork circle on the south coast of England. This former Anglo-Saxon fort is located at the nodal intersection of five ley lines. On August 25, 1974, William Lincoln was lifted five feet up into the air here, and suspended horizontally for thirty seconds before returning to the ground. Three of his friends witnessed this event.

---

4   J. Michell, *The New View Over Atlantis* (San Francisco: Harper & Row, 1983).

The secret alliance

It would be almost impossible for time travelers to have any significant effect on our civilization without forging an alliance with our government. The United States is their current experiment. As we have already seen, a secret alliance has been formed between the time travelers and our military.

Certain military bases in the Southwest are used to conduct experiments, and this is where these chrononauts give us advanced technology. In Colorado, Utah, New Mexico, Arizona, and Nevada there are secret bases built by our government specifically for this exchange that are under the direction of the time travelers. Consider also the unmarked helicopters that are seen by abductees for months following their experiments.

Time travelers have been in direct contact with our species for at least 25,000 years! They created all of our religious governments, and directed our art, music, and literature, all for the purpose of enhancing our growth. The problem is that our forefathers became power-hungry and greedy, and distorted these well-meaning attempts at civilizing us. Throughout history secret alliances have been made with governments, religious leaders, and the corporate world.

Never underestimate the willingness of our government, and those of other nations, to cut deals with advanced intelligences and hide their behavior from the public. All of these secret alliances were nothing more than experiments that failed.

Chapter 9

Our own time traveling

In voyaging through time there are certain rules and limitations you need to be aware of. Here are some principles that reflect my training of more than 11,000 patients in the art of time travel, as well as my own personal time excursions.

- There are only certain time periods and locations you are capable of visiting. Due to your own karmic growth as a soul and so that you don't interfere with the universe's overall plan, some dates and places are beyond your grasp.

- It is difficult to specifically go to an exact time, as time travel appears quite sporadic. For example, you may easily move ahead three days in time, but have great difficulty in viewing an occurrence one hour in the future.

- These "windows in time" are unique to each individual. Some people find it easy to travel 500 or 1,000 years back or forward in time, but considerably shorter time intervals are out of their reach.

- Traveling back in time several hundred years to a scene that takes only a few seconds of time in that bygone era requires perhaps several minutes in the present time frame.

- Going into the future by five or six hundred years to an episode that encompasses several weeks in, for example, the twenty-sixth century requires only a few minutes in the present to explore.

- Colors appear duller as we voyage back in time. A black-and-white monochrome-like effect is commonly observed if we travel great distances back in time.

- Traveling into the future results in a sharpening of color perception. The farther ahead in time we travel, the more brilliant these colors appear. Placing ourselves in the twenty-eighth century may very well result in a psychedelic display of colors. This paradigm may also apply to our other senses.

- With experience you can control your time traveling to the extent that it can assist your personal or professional life. For instance, these techniques can be used to go into the future by one day to view a business meeting or social date. You not only have the opportunity to overview this exchange, but may be able to maximize your goal because that individual will now feel more comfortable with you, since he or she will have a feeling that they have met you before.

- Always maintain a high code of ethics when using time travel exercises. Never attempt to manipulate others through time travel. Any such unethical motives will be noted by the universe and karmic laws are such that you will lose in the long run.

There is nothing wrong with benefiting materially or in any other way. You may use these techniques to find a soul mate, improve your health, or advance your career. Just refrain from accomplishing these goals at the expense of someone else. "What goes around comes around" is the karmic principle to always bear in mind.

In this chapter are several hypnotic techniques. If you feel a little anxious about practicing self-hypnosis exercises, try this simple breathing technique first.

1. While sitting up straight, place your left hand on your abdomen and right hand on your chest.

2. Inhale slowly and deeply. Visualize your lungs filling with air from the bottom up, so that your left hand rises before your right hand does.

3. Exhale slowly, reversing the process by emptying your lungs from the top down.

This method can quickly help dissipate stress at any time of the day. I highly recommend you practice breathing slowly from the deep bottom of your lungs up, for two to five minutes at least once each day.

Age regression

For those of you who would like to explore a previous abduction and contact with these chrononauts, try the following simple self-hypnosis exercise. (For convenience, you may want to make a tape recording of this script.)

> Now listen very carefully. I want you to imagine a bright white light coming down from above and entering the top of your head. Filling your entire body. See it, feel it and it becomes reality. Now imagine an aura of pure white light emanating from your heart region. Again surrounding your entire body. Protecting you. See it, feel it, and it becomes reality. Now only your masters and guides and highly evolved loving entities who mean you well will be able to influence you during this or any other hypnotic session. You are totally protected by this aura of pure white light.

As I count backward from 20 to 1, you are going to perceive yourself moving through a very deep and dark tunnel. The tunnel will get lighter and lighter and at the very end of this tunnel there will be a door with a bright white light above it. When you walk through this door you will be at an earlier age. You're going to re-experience this earlier age and move to an event that will be significant in explaining your present personality, or the origin of any problem or negative tendency.

If you have ever been abducted, or had any type of contact with an advanced being of any kind, you will be able to recall the details of the circumstances comfortably and with complete safety. If you feel uncomfortable either physically, mentally, or emotionally at any time you can awaken yourself form this hypnotic trance by simply counting forward from 1 to 5. You will always associate my voice as a friendly voice in trance. You will be able to let your mind review back into its memory banks and follow the instructions of perceiving the scenes from this earlier age and follow along as I instruct. You'll find yourself able to get more quickly and deeply into hypnotic trances each time you practice with this tape or other methods of self-hypnosis. When you hear me say the words "sleep now and rest," I want you to immediately detach yourself from any scene you are experiencing. You will be able to wait for further instructions.

You absolutely have the power and ability to go back in time as your subconscious mind's memory bank remembers everything you've ever experienced. I want you to relive these past events only as a neutral observer without feeling or emotion, just as if you were watching a television show. You will be able to remove any obstacles that are preventing you from achieving your most useful, positive, beneficial, and constructive goals. Go back and be able to explore at least two or three memories of yourself. It doesn't matter how far you go back. It doesn't matter what the years are.

I'm going to count backward now from 20 to 1. As I do so, I want you to feel yourself moving into the past. You'll find yourself moving through a pitch black tunnel that will get lighter and lighter as I count backward. When I reach the count of 1 you will have opened up a door with a bright white light above it and walked into a past scene. You will once again become yourself at an earlier age. Now listen carefully. Number 20, you're moving into a very deep dark tunnel, surrounded by grass and trees and flowers and a very inviting atmosphere. You feel calm and comfortable about moving into the tunnel, 19, 18 you're moving backward in time, back, back, 17, 16, 15 the tunnel is becoming lighter now. You can make out your arms and legs and you realize that you are walking through this tunnel and you're moving backward in time. 14, 13, 12 moving so far back, back, 11, 10, 9 you're so far back now you're over halfway there—the tunnel is much lighter. You can perceive things around you and you can now make out the door in front of you with the bright white light above it. 8, 7, 6 standing in front of the door now feeling comfortable and feeling positive and confident about your ability to move into this past scene. 5, 4 now walk up to the door, put your hand on the doorknob. The bright white light is so bright it's hard to look at. 3 open the door, 2 step through the door, 1 move into the past scene. You are there.

Focus carefully on what you see before you. Take a few minutes now and I want you to let everything become crystal clear.

The information flowing into your awareness is of the scene becoming visual and visible. Just let yourself orient to your environment. Focus on it. Take a few moments and then listen to my instructions. Let the impressions form.

Play New Age music for 30 seconds.

First, what do you perceive and what are you doing? Focus carefully on my voice now. I want you to let any information about the scene, as well as the actual environment that you are in, flow into your awareness and become clear now. Crystal clear. I want you to focus on yourself. Focus first of all on where you are, focus on how old you are, how you are dressed, what you are doing there, what your purpose is there at this particular time, who else is around you—parents, relatives, friends. If you were abducted, move to the very first time this incident occurred. Let the scene develop, develop and become clear.

Play New Age music for 4 minutes.

Sleep now and rest. Detach yourself from this scene now. I want you now to focus on my voice again. I'm going to be counting forward this time from 1 to 5. When I reach the count of 5, I want you to progress in time by three years. I want you to move at least three years farther forward in time. Moving to a specific event that is going to happen to you. Something that is going to affect you and your development. I want you to move forward to a very significant scene. This may be another abduction. On the count of 5 now I want you to perceive yourself in this scene just like you did before. Number 1, moving forward, carefully, comfortably, slowly. Number 2, moving farther forward. Number 3, halfway there, 4 almost there, 5 you are there. Now focus again, let the scene crystalize, become clear. Focus on yourself. Where you are. Who you are with. What is happening around you. What has happened since I last spoke with you. Understand the physical setting of the scene. Let it develop. Allow it to relate to your particular problem or just to experience going back in time. Carefully, comfortably allow the scene to unfold. Carefully and comfortably. Now perceive the scene unfold. Let it unfold now.

Play New Age music for 4 minutes.

Sleep now and rest. Listen to my voice and detach yourself from this scene. We're going to be moving forward one more time now. On the count of 5 you're going to be moving forward to a minimum of five years from this time. You will be moving forward to what will ideally be the resolution to this problem or another significant scene that will affect the development of this problem, and recall in detail any messages or instructions given to you by advanced beings. Now move forward on the count of 5. Number 1 moving forward, 2 moving farther forward, 3 half way there, 4 almost there, 5. Now again let the scene crystalize, become crystal clear. Focus on what is happening around you. Where you are, who you are with, what has happened since I last spoke with you, and if this is a problem you are resolving, exactly what happened, exactly how it was resolved. Find out what additional facts are related to the present problem. Carefully and comfortably let the images flow and any messages become clear. Do this now.

Play New Age music for 4 minutes.

All right, very good, you've done very well now. Sleep now and rest. Listen carefully as I am going to count forward again from 1 to 5. On the count of 5 you will be back in the present.

You will still be in a deep hypnotic trance, but you will be able to relax comfortably and be free of these scenes. You will still be in trance. Number 1, you're heading forward in time to the present, 2 farther forward, 3 halfway there, 4 almost there, number 5. Listen as I count forward one more time from 1 to 5. On the count of 5 you will be wide awake, refreshed, relaxed—you will be able to do what you have planned for the rest of the day or evening. You will be able to remember every thing that you experienced and re-experienced, and be perfectly relaxed and at ease. You will also be able to facilitate further experiences of scenes from the past with additional playing of this tape. Number 1 very, very deep, 2 you're getting a little lighter, 3 you're getting much much lighter, 4 very, very light, 5 awaken.

Past life regression

We can use hypnosis to travel back in time to lives we lived in centuries past. This is called past life regression. Age regression is simply going back in time to an earlier stage of our current lifetime. I use age regression in my work as a forensic expert in criminal and civil cases, in addition to abduction cases and assisting patients in locating lost items.

Here is a case that does not appear in any of my books. Several years ago a woman named Suzette came to my Los Angeles office from her home in Paris. She had read my first book, *Past Lives—Future Lives,* and wanted to find out the origin of her fear of meeting new people.

In a past life in ancient Rome, Suzette was a male named Julius who earned a meager living as a shopkeeper's assistant. One of his friends convinced Julius to team up with him as a preacher of sorts. This was shortly after Christianity was made the official religion of the Roman Empire (fourth century A.D.).

Julius was not very skilled at preaching, nor did he properly prepare his sermons. One evening an unruly crowd of parishioners vehemently objected to Julius' sermon and stoned him to death. Needless to say, Suzette was quite surprised by this scenario. She expected a past life in which she was a ballet dancer or singer with a poor performance to coincide with her malady. The last thing she expected to perceive herself as was an incompetent male preacher.

Some of the regressions I have performed on my patients have dated as far back as four million years ago! Past life regression is not limited to a certain type of individual. We have all had past lives and we will all live in future time eras in a new body.

If you would like to review one of your past lives to see if abductions have established a karmic pattern, try this exercise:

Now listen very carefully. I want you to imagine a bright white light coming down from above and entering the top of your head. Filling your entire body. See it, feel it, and it becomes reality. Now imagine an aura of pure white light emanating from your heart region. Again surrounding your entire body. Protecting you. See it, feel it and it becomes reality. Now only your masters and guides and highly evolved loving entities who mean you well will be able to influence you during this or any other hypnotic session. You are totally protected by this aura of pure white light. Now listen very carefully; in a few minutes I'm going to be counting backward from 20 to 1. As I count backward from 20 to 1 you are going to perceive yourself moving through a very deep and dark tunnel. The tunnel will get lighter and lighter and at the very end of this tunnel there will be a door with a bright white light above it. When you walk through this door you will be in a past life scene. You're going to re-experience one of your past lives at the age of about fifteen. You'll be moving to an event that will be significant in explaining who you are, where you are, and why you are there. I want you to realize that if you feel uncomfortable either physically, mentally or emotionally at any time you can awaken yourself from this hypnotic trance by simply counting forward from 1 to 5. You will always associate my voice as a friendly voice in trance. You will be able to let your mind review its memory banks and follow the instructions to perceive the scenes of your own past lives and follow along as I instruct. You'll find yourself able to get deeper and more quickly into hypnotic trances each time as you practice with this tape or other methods of self-hypnosis. When you hear me say the words "sleep now and rest," I want you to immediately detach yourself from any scene you are experiencing. You will be able to wait for further instructions.

You absolutely have the power and ability to go back into a past life as your subconscious mind's memory bank remembers everything you've ever experienced in all your past lives as well as your present life. I want you to relive these past life events only as a neutral observer, without feeling or emotion, just as if you were watching a television show. I want you to choose a past life now in which you've lived to at least the age of thirty. I want you to select a past life when you had contact with a superior being not from your society. If you were abducted during this lifetime, you will be able to explore it safely and with complete memories upon returning to normal consciousness. I'm going to count backward now from 20 to 1. As I do so I want you to feel yourself moving into the past. You'll find yourself moving through a pitch black tunnel that will get lighter and lighter as I count backward. When I reach the count of 1 you will have opened up a door with a bright white light above it and walked into a past life scene. You will once again become yourself at about the age of fifteen in a previous lifetime. Now listen carefully. Number 20 you're moving into a very deep dark tunnel surrounded by grass and trees and your favorite flowers. You feel very calm and comfortable about moving into the tunnel. 19, 18 you're moving backward in time, back, back, 17, 16, 15 the tunnel is becoming lighter now. You can make out your arms and legs and you realize that you are walking through this tunnel and moving backward in time. 14, 13, 12 moving so far back, back, back, 11, 10, 9 you're now so far back—you're over halfway there, the tunnel is much lighter. You can see around you and you can now make out the door in front of you with the bright white light above it. 8, 7, 6 standing in front of the door now feeling comfortable and positive and confident about your ability to move into this past life scene. 5, 4, now walk up to the door, put your hand on the doorknob; the bright white light is so bright it's hard to look at. 3 open the door, 2 step through the door, 1 move into the past life scene. Focus carefully on what you perceive before you. Take a few minutes now and let everything become crystal clear. The information flowing into your awareness makes the scene visible. Just let yourself orient to your new environment. Focus on it. Take a few moments and listen to my instructions. Let the impression form. First what do you see and what are you doing? Are you male or female? Look at your feet first—what type of footwear or shoes are you wearing? Now move up the body and see exactly how you are clothed. How old are you? What are you doing right now? What is happening around you? Describe the situation you find yourself in. Are you outdoors or indoors? Is it day or night? Is it hot or cold?

night? Is it hot or cold? What country or land do you live in or are you from? Now focus on this one carefully—what do people call you? What is the year? Take a few moments and numbers may appear right in front of your awareness. You will be informed what year this is. Take a few more moments to let any additional information crystalize and become clear into your awareness about the environment that you find yourself in. Take a few moments. Let any additional information be made clear to you.

Play New Age music for 3 minutes.

Very good now. Listen very carefully to my voice now. Sleep now and rest. Detach yourself from this scene just for a moment. I'm going to be counting forward from 1 to 5. When I reach the count of 5 you're going to be moving forward now to a significant event that's going to occur in this lifetime that will affect you personally. It will also most probably affect those close to you—it may involve your parents, friends—people who are close to you in this lifetime. If you have ever been abducted in this past life, move to this incident now. Focus carefully now. Sleep now and rest and listen now as I count forward from 1 to 5. On the count of 5 you will be moving forward in time to a significant event that is going to occur to you. 1 moving forward, slowing, carefully, comfortably, 2 feeling good as you move forward in time, 3 halfway there, 4 almost there, 5. Now again focus on yourself and the environment you find yourself in. What are you doing now and why are you in this environment? Has anything changed since I last spoke with you? What is happening around you? Are there any other people around you who are important to you? If there are, are they male or female? Are they friends or relatives? How do they relate to you? Why are they important to you? Focus on your clothes now, starting with your feet first. How are you dressed? Are you dressed any differently than when I last spoke with you? Move all the way up your body and perceive how you are dressed. Then look at the people next to you. Are they dressed any differently? About how old are you now? Focus on that for a moment—a number will appear to you—about how old are you right now? Where exactly are you? Are you out-doors or indoors? Is it day or night? What season is this? What kind of occupation do you have? What do you do to pass the time? What do you do with your day? Focus on how you spend your time. Now I want you to focus on an event that's going to be happening right now that you find yourself right in the middle of. I want you to take this event right through to com-pletion. If this is an abduction, let all of the details unfold safe-ly and comfortably. Take a few moments and carry this event through to completion.

Play New Age music for 3 minutes.

All right now. Sleep now and rest. Detach yourself from this scene you are experiencing and listen to my voice again. You're going to be moving forward now by a period as long as neces-sary but a minimum of three years. You will not have died. It will be at least three years farther in time. Now I want you to move forward to a significant event that is going to affect not only the kind of work that you do but also yourself personally. It may even be another abduction. I want you to move forward to this very significant time, at least three years from now. On the count of 5 move forward very carefully and comfortably. 1

almost there, 5. Now what do you perceive around you? What has transpired since I last saw you? Focus on yourself first. Perceive where you are, how you are dressed, what environment you are in, where you are located if it was a different physical environment, and who you are with. Take a few moments and let this information crystalize and become clear into your awareness.

Play New Age music for 3 minutes.

All right now. Sleep now and rest. Detach yourself from this scene. We're going to be moving forward again on the count of 5. This time you're going to be moving forward to a scene that will signify or illustrate the maximum achievements you have accomplished in this lifetime, personally or professionally. You'll be surrounded by the people that affect you most in this lifetime. You will be achieving the maximum amount of success or goals or whatever else you wanted to accomplish in this lifetime. You will remember any communication from any strange or more advanced beings. Move forward to this maximum accomplishment in this lifetime, on the count of 5. 1 moving forward slowly, carefully, comfortably, 2 moving further forward, 3 halfway there, 4 almost there, 5. Now take a few moments and see where you find yourself. What is your environment? What has happened and why is this time of your life so important to you? Focus on it and see what you've accomplished, and let all the information be made clear to you.

Play New Age music for 3 minutes.

Now that you've been able to perceive this particular period of your life I want you to evaluate your life. I want you to find out what goals you were supposed to accomplish and what out what goals you were supposed to accomplish and what you actually did accomplish. What do you feel that you learned from this lifetime? What do you feel that you have gained from this lifetime in your own personal goals, family life, or relationships? Let the information flow—what did you gain? Now let's focus on what you weren't able to achieve. Focus on what you felt you would have liked more time for. What do you feel you weren't able to accomplish and why? Focus on that. Let the information flow. Remember, in this particular lifetime you are still alive now. I want you now to focus on your activities—whatever you're doing in this particular scene—to evaluate why this lifetime was important to you. What necessary or needed experience did you gain from this lifetime? Focus on this now. Let the information flow into your awareness.

Play New Age music for 3 minutes.

All right now. Sleep now and rest. You did very very well. Listen very carefully. I'm going to count forward now from 1 to 5, one more time. This time when I reach 5 you will be back in the present, you will be able to remember everything you experienced and re-experienced, you'll feel very relaxed, refreshed, and you'll be able to do whatever you have planned for the rest of the day or evening. You'll feel very positive about what you've just experienced and very motivated about your confidence and ability to experience additional lifetimes. All right now. 1 very, very deep, 2 you're getting a little bit lighter, 3 you're getting much, much lighter, 4 very very light, 5 awaken. Wide awake and refreshed.

Time travel on the other side

There are three types of out-of-body experiences (OBEs). We are familiar with the near-death experiences (NDEs) first reported by Dr. Raymond Moody in his 1975 book *Life After Life*.[1] This temporary clinical death of the individual sometimes imparts information about the patient's future.

The Three Mile Island nuclear plant meltdown and the eruption of Mount St. Helens are two examples of documented precognitions resulting from NDEs.[2] NDEs cannot be attributed to cultural conditioning, drugs, or hallucinations. They transform the personality of the recipient so that increased compassion, improved self-confidence, and greater zest for life are seen following this phenomenon.

The problem with an NDE is that you must be clinically dead to experience this trip into the future. A regular OBE, such as runner's hypnosis, all dreams, deep levels of hypnosis, meditation, yoga, and so on, also occasionally produces an excursion into the future. This is the second type of OBE.

The last type of OBE is a form of leaving the physical body that I term the conscious out-of-body experience (COBE). This consists of an OBE during which we can merge with our Higher Self (the white light) at the moment of physical death and perfect our soul, thus eliminating the need to reincarnate. I call this ascension technique *conscious dying*.[2]

In all three types of OBEs, our subconscious mind is now located in the astral plane, where all past, present, and future events can be viewed simultaneously. All communication is by telepathy, and there is no time as we know it on the physical plane. My patients have been able to perceive former lives, the earlier stages of their current life (age regression), the future of their present incarnation (age progression), and future lives during these astral voyages. This is the closest experience to the eternal now that our soul may achieve until it eventually perfects its energy and ascends to the God plane.

---

1   R. Moody, *Life After Life* (New York: Bantam, 1975).
2   Goldberg, *Peaceful Transition* (1997), p. 16.

Dreams of the future

It is well established in scientific literature that any type of altered state of consciousness (ASC) may produce precognitive experiences. Dreams are another example of an ASC.

The parapsychological researcher Hans Holzer breaks down dreams into six categories.[3] These may be described as follows:

- **Survival dreams**—A discarnate entity or spirit communicates with us in this dream type.

- **Reincarnation dreams**—Voyages into either past or future lives comprise this category. (See my books, *Past Lives—Future Lives, The Search for Grace,* and *Soul Healing* for a thorough discussion of this concept and dozens of case histories.)

- **ESP dreams**—Psychic talents, such as precognition, telepathy, and clairvoyance, may be exhibited during this dream type.

- **Out-of-body experiences (OBEs)**—All dreams represent OBEs. Astral projection and lucid dreams are examples of this genre.

- **Warning dreams**—When we receive a changeable future event in a dream, a warning dream is the term we use to describe this natural excursion.

- **Prophetic dreams**—A futuristic dream that we do not appear to be able to alter is a prophetic dream.

Two major theories have been postulated to explain precognitive dreams. One approach views the future as already existing in a complete form, not unlike our present. This suggests predestination and goes against my entire clinical experience, as well as quantum physics. The second explanation considers the future as "plastic." Our actions alter this potential future and parallel universes exist for us to occupy at the same time.

A skeptical and conventional scientist might attempt to explain precognition as a form of déjà vu or paramnesia (a defect in memory

---

3   H. Holzer, *The Psychic Side of Dreams* (St. Paul: Llewellyn, 1994).

during which the individual experiences a confused sense of time). Cases of double déjà vu, in which two people experience the same precognitive dream, should put this antiquated theory to rest once and for all.

To be classified as a precognitive dream, the information received could not have been acquired through any of our five senses. Data we obtain that result from a cognitive overview of the circumstances by interpreting known past events or through previous knowledge cannot be accurately labeled as precognitive.

The shorter the time interval between the precognitive dream and the probable event, the greater the chance that the dream will be accurate in our conscious awareness. Of course, conscious action can alter the outcome of these futuristic depictions. To do this we would have to move into a parallel universe.

Using age progression (see script of hypnotic age progression technique at the end of this chapter) allows us an untapped form of psychic empowerment. There are no limitations to what the subconscious can accomplish if it is properly trained.

To understand precognition, consider the following. In precognition we are confronted with the effect before the cause, indicating that the mind can be as independent of TIME and it can be of SPACE. But cause and effect cannot exist apart from SPACE and TIME, because space and time do not exist as independent entities. There is a limit to human thought, because the implications of SPACE-TIME are only imperfectly understood. Human beings are simultaneously inhabitants of the world of space and time and the continuum of SPACE-TIME. Our conception of TIME is due to a structure of our minds which can deal only with a three-dimensional world. SPACE-TIME is a continuum of four dimensions, which is difficult to imagine.

When we experience REM (rapid eye movements characteristic of dreams) during our sleep cycle, our mind moves backward and forward in time. There is no sense of time at the very deepest level of consciousness. Only an eternal now exists, during which all events coexist in the space-time continuum.

Time travel case histories through dreams

In 1985 one of my patients named Mildred completed her hypnotherapy with me in just a few visits. She was fascinated with age progression, successfully perceiving her five frequencies and selecting her ideal frequency.

Several months later, events transpired that proved to her she was on her ideal path, but this case took an unusual turn in 1986. One night she went to bed quite late and had what she thought was a most unusual dream.

In this "dream" she saw herself in Texas visiting her parents. The television news reported that it was October 4, 1988, not 1986. During this time travel experience Mildred felt uncomfortable about this date and checked various publications (newspapers, magazines, the TV guide, etc.) to confirm the date. They all reinforced the fact that it was October 4, 1988.

Mildred's parents commented on her unexplained anxiety during this visit. To prove to herself this was a dream, Mildred went into her parents' backyard and buried in a coffee can a note she wrote to herself stating that it was really October 4, 1986. She included the masthead from that day's Texas newspaper showing it to be October 4, 1988.

When she awoke the following morning, Mildred immediately picked up the newspaper delivered to her home and checked the date. It read October 5, 1986. Later that evening she called her parents and asked them if anything unusual had happened the previous day. They stated that everything was normal.

Mildred asked them when they last saw her and her parents responded that it was about six months ago. All this appeared to coincide with Mildred's memory. Mildred did not visit her parents for another eighteen months, but they made several trips to her home in Washington, D.C.

By the time Mildred again visited her parents' home it was April of 1988. This trip was uneventful. Mildred checked her parents' backyard for the coffee can, but it was not to be found. The following trip was during Thanksgiving at the end of November of 1988. During this trip she again went into the backyard with her parents, after explaining this most unusual dream.

They watched as Mildred unearthed the coffee can. Mildred instructed them to take out the contents. The note dated October 4, 1986, along with the October 4, 1988, newspaper masthead, were found in the can.

A most puzzling look was exchanged between her parents. Their question to Mildred concerned why she hadn't stayed for a visit when she came to Texas the previous month. Mildred patiently informed them that the last time she was in the state was in April of that year. To this day her parents refuse to discuss this incident.

What apparently occurred was that Mildred went into the future on the same frequency she occupied on October 4, 1986 and buried the coffee can. By October 1988 she had switched tracks to a different parallel universe and did not make the trip to Texas on this frequency.

By the following month Mildred had again switched back to her 1986 frequency and was able to uncover the coffee can that she buried two years before.

My own precognitive dream while driving

My own trip into the future occurred while driving to Ft. Lauderdale, Florida, from the University of Maryland School of Dentistry when I was a student there back in the early 1970s. Since Christmas vacation represented the only significant break until the summer, I looked forward to these trips.

My method of maximizing this vacation time consisted of driving straight to Florida from Baltimore, stopping only four times for gas on the 1,000-mile trip. This particular trip was significant because, while driving in the very early hours of the morning, I nearly dozed off on the highway. Occasionally a jolting sensation sharpened my conscious awareness.

The next thing I was aware of was arriving in Florida, renting a room in a private residence and being frustrated at not being able to fall asleep due to my now-alert mind. I noticed an unusual design of the wallpaper in the room as I lay on the bed trying to provide my fatigued body with its needed rest. I did eventually fall asleep.

Back on the highway, I was jolted back into a hyper-alert consciousness and completed my trip. My first thought was, "Did I dream that scene or did I really go into the future?" The difference between this being a mere dream or a teleportation into the future occurred to me several hours later.

Upon arrival in Ft. Lauderdale every detail of my "dream" manifested into reality. When I purchased a paper, I haphazardly called the telephone number from an ad showing a room to rent in a private home. After arriving at this house I dragged my fatigued body to the bed and found it difficult to sleep, since my mind was still in a hyper-alert state. Last, I noticed the wallpaper of the bedroom bearing the same unusual design I had "seen" on the highway in Georgia several hours before! I had never been to this house before.

My explanation for this event involves two important principles. First, I did literally see into the future and remained on that same parallel universe or frequency. Second, this experience most likely was an out-of-body experience or astral projection, since my landlord did not appear to recognize me the "second" time he saw me.

Age progression

The term "age progression" is preferable to "precognition" in describing moving forward in time with hypnosis. Many people consider precognition to be a unique mystical experience, and find the expression "age progression" easier to relate to.

Two exercises for progressing into the future will be presented in this chapter, but first let us consider some examples of individuals who have traveled into the future of their current life and into a future lifetime.

Novels that foretell the future

Under the pen name of Harrison James, James Rusk, Jr. in 1972 wrote a novel titled *Black Abductor*, published by Regency Press. This book depicted a group of terrorists led by a black man who kidnaps the daughter of a wealthy and famous man with strong right-wing sympathies.

Patricia is abducted near her college. Her boyfriend is beaten by the criminals and is initially a suspect in the case. Patricia at first resists her captors, but eventually joins their cause. Photographs of her are sent to her father. At the end of this novel the kidnappers are surrounded by police, tear-gassed, and killed.

In 1974 Patricia Hearst, the college-student daughter of the wealthy and famous right-wing media magnate William Randolph Hearst, was kidnapped near her college by members of the Symbionese Liberation Army. This terrorist group had a black leader.

The FBI initially suspected Patricia's former boyfriend, Steven Weed, who was with her during her abduction and was badly beaten, but eventually removed him as a suspect. Another interesting coincidence was that the terrorists were surrounded by the police, tear-gassed, and killed.[4] Did James Rusk, Jr. somehow peer into the future to perceive these events and report them two years before they happened?

Cyrano de Bergerac

We are all familiar with the prophecies of Nostradamus, Edgar Cayce, Jeanne Dixon, and the futuristic visions of Leonardo da Vinci. Not so well known are the visions of the future of the French author Savinien Cyrano de Bergerac.

Edmond Rostand's play depicts de Bergerac as an excellent swordsman, who tries to win the heart of a lady. De Bergerac wrote two books, *Voyages to the Moon* and *Voyages to the Sun,* that were published after his death, in 1656 and 1662 respectively, and later combined in one volume.

The book theorizes the orbit of the Earth and other planets around the Sun (not a popular position at that time, as Galileo found out during the Inquisition), and the weak gravitational field of the Moon. De Bergerac's theory that the gods of the ancients were actually travelers from outer space was published more than 300 years before Erich von Däniken's first book was published.

---

4   A. Vaughan, *Incredible Coincidence* (New York: J. B. Lippincott Company, 1979) pp. 55–56.

De Bergerac described radiant bulbs that made the lunar night as bright as day, and devices that recorded and played back human voices. He also pictured houses that moved around with the seasons. Light bulbs, tape recorders, and mobile homes were not even entertained as possible inventions in Cyrano's time. This may well be another example of time travel into the future.

Jules Verne

Another French novelist of international renown was Jules Verne. His novel *From the Earth to the Moon,* appeared in 1865. Verne's description of this trip showed amazing similarity to Apollo 11's maiden voyage to the Moon. There are some striking similarities:

- The initial breakaway velocity of Jules Verne's craft was 36,000 feet per second while Apollo 11's third-stage velocity was 35,533 feet per second.

- The huge cannon which fired Verne's capsule into space was called the Columbiad, while Apollo 11's was named Columbia.

- Both capsules orbited the Moon several times, occasionally at the same altitude. Both teams took photographs and the Verne capsule crew even charted the Sea of Tranquility where the Apollo 11 crew landed.

- The launch sites were almost identical. Verne chose a spot in Florida about 140 miles due west of Cape Kennedy. In Verne's story, Texas fought for the honor—today's Mission Control Center is in Houston, Texas.

- Verne's capsule reached the moon in 97 hours 13 minutes, while Apollo's time was 103 hours 30 minutes. In Verne's ship there were three men, two Americans and a Frenchman. Apollo 11 had a crew of three also.

- Verne's "space capsule" was 15 feet high by 9 feet in diameter, the Apollo command module 10½ feet high and 12 feet 10 inches in diameter.

- Both capsules splashed down in the Pacific and both crews were picked up by the American Navy ships.

What explanation, other than time travel, could possibly account for these similarities? I suspect the odds would be millions to one of these hits being registered 104 years ahead of time.

H. G. Wells and the fifth dimension

This section would not be complete without commenting on the work of the British novelist H. G. Wells. In 1896 he wrote a short work of fiction that appeared in a British magazine called *The New Review*. Wells' story dealt with a chemistry teacher named Plattner, whose experiments with a strange green powder result in an explosion transporting Plattner into the fifth dimension.

This story, titled "The Plattner Story," describes Plattner's voyage to a shadowy world with a green sun. Its inhabitants are strange creatures known as the "Watchers of the Living," who spend their time looking into our world. The chemist finally is successful in creating a second explosion that returns him to nineteenth-century England. The importance of this story is that it was the first appearance in popular fiction of the fifth dimension.

A Pre-World War II flight four years ahead of time

In 1934 Victor Goddard was caught in a storm over Scotland. The Royal Air Force pilot desperately sought a landmark that would allow him to get his bearings, as he was lost. Goddard deduced that he was near Drem, the location of an abandoned airfield.

As the Hawker Hart biplane descended through the clouds he was pleased to see landmarks indicating he was in Drem. He soon came upon the airfield, but an unusual thing occurred. Sir Goddard later described this as "Suddenly the area was bathed in an ethereal light as though the sun were shining on a midsummer day."[5]

Instead of a deserted airport, it was a hive of activity. Goddard observed mechanics in blue overalls working on yellow planes. Although he flew at an altitude of only 50 feet, surprisingly nobody

---

5   A. Hall, *Signs of Things to Come* (London: Aldus Books Ltd., 1975), p. 17.

looked up as his plane flew by. Victor Goddard immediately headed back into the clouds as he regained his bearings.

Goddard's confusion resurfaced in 1938 when the abandoned airport in Drem was reopened with war on the horizon. The Drem airport was transformed into an air force flying school. Interestingly, the color of British training planes was changed from the previous silver color to yellow.

The ethereal light may have been a portal in time that projected Victor Goddard four years into the future for a brief visit. This light could have been one indication of entering hyperspace and traveling through hyperspace on the way to the future. This reminds me of the white light phenomenon reported in near-death experiences, during which information from the future is sometimes reported.

A time traveler saves her life by seeing a possible future

A young woman named Tami, whom I trained in the art of time travel, had just graduated from college. She planned to join some of her college friends in Paris that summer, flying there from New York on July 17, 1996, on flight 800.

Before making this reservation, she practiced her time travel techniques and voyaged into the future. Tami was shocked to discover that had she boarded this plane, she would have died as a result of a plane crash. Not willing to risk her life, she booked a later flight.

On July 17, 1996, TWA flight 800 crashed, killing all of its 230 passengers and crew. Tami saved her own life by utilizing the principles of quantum physics and age progression. She changed her frequency and lived to talk about it. According to quantum physics, Tami did die on at least one parallel universe. However, you can't convince her of that theoretical paradigm.

A television newscaster documents his age progressions

Many people are skeptical about the validity of progressing into the future through hypnosis, or by any other means. To demonstrate how uncannily accurate hypnotic age progression can be, I applied this technique with a television newscaster who hosted a noon news show (reported in my first book, *Past Lives—Future Lives*).

Earlier I had successfully regressed newscaster Harry Martin into three of his previous lifetimes. Harry would receive his assignments and the itinerary for his show on an assignment board in the newsroom, so I had him read this board in trance seven to ten days in the future!

Amazingly, Harry reported nine different news items. One item pinpointed an accident between two vehicles on the northwestern section of the Baltimore Beltway (highway 695). This did indeed occur exactly one week from the date of this progression.

Another hit involved a fire in a row house in Baltimore. Harry gave me the name of a neighbor (Johnson) who was later interviewed by the media about this incident.

Under hypnosis, Harry read off to me nine news items from the futuristic assignment board. Six of these nine items matched the actual occurrence. Four of the six "hits" were exactly one week in the future, the other two were three and five days prior to their realization.

The three items that were misses can simply be explained as taking place on a different frequency or parallel universe. If this data were mere speculation or confabulation, no hits would have been observed. Harry's attitude concerning progression was skeptical. Belief in the theory is not necessary for it to work.

An exercise in age progression

The self-hypnosis technique that follows will enable you to travel into the future. To obtain the most benefit from this experience, I suggest you make a tape of the script beginning on page 182, or you can obtain professionally recorded cassette tapes through either Llewellyn Worldwide or my office.

There are certain principles you may wish to adhere to when practicing age progression:

- Try to eliminate preconceptions of how you expect the future to appear.

- Information you receive at first may not seem to originate from the future. By refraining from analyzing these data, you will allow your subconscious to present the future in its own way.

- There are various ways in which you may receive a future frequency. You may have a sense of "just knowing," a visual scene, data alone, words spoken in your "inner ear," or a flash of information appearing before your "inner eyes." Just relax and let this information manifest itself.

- For those of you concerned about receiving "forbidden knowledge," let me assure you that no technique can violate a universal law. Any information you obtain is within your karmic rights.

Here is a simple exercise to help you perceive your five frequencies:

1. Take a deep breath and hold it to the count of eight. Let it out slowly and visualize a series of five doors, each with the word "Future" printed on it in large bold letters. These doors are numbered 1 through 5.

2. Think of a situation or upcoming event that you would like to explore. Gather the actual facts you currently have available on this circumstance and review them in your mind.

3. Now open up the door labeled Future 1 and perceive how this situation will unfold. Observe as many details as you can. Refrain from getting emotionally involved with this option.

4. Repeat this procedure for the doors labeled Future 2, Future 3, Future 4, and Future 5.

5. Choose the door that best meets your needs and meditate on the number of that door for two minutes.

You have just perceived your parallel universe options and programmed yourself to switch tracks to that desired frequency.

With this background you are now ready to practice a complete age progression exercise:

Now listen very carefully. I want you to imagine a bright white light coming down from above and entering the top of your head, filling your entire body. See it, feel it, and it becomes reality. Now imagine an aura of pure white light emanating from your heart region, again surrounding your entire body, protecting you. See it, feel it, and it becomes a reality. Now only your higher self, masters and guides, and highly evolved loving entities who mean you well will be able to influence you during this or any other hypnotic session. You are totally protected by this aura of pure white light. Focus carefully on my voice as your subconscious mind's memory bank has memories of all past, present, and future events. This tape will help guide you into the future and a dream of a future event today that will facilitate your spiritual growth. Shortly I am going to be counting forward from 1 to 20. Near the end of this count you are going to imagine yourself moving through a tunnel. Near the end of this count you will perceive the tunnel divide and veer off to the left and to the right. The right represents the past, the left represents the future. On the count of 20 you will perceive yourself in the future. Your subconscious and superconscious mind levels have all the knowledge and information that you desire. Carefully and comfortably feel yourself moving into the future with each count from 1 to 20. Listen carefully now.

Number 1, feel yourself now moving forward to the future, into this very, very deep and dark tunnel. 2, 3 farther and farther and farther in to the future. It is a little bit disorienting, but you know you're moving into the future. 4, 5, 6, 7, 8, 9 it's more stable now and you feel comfortable, you feel almost as if you're floating, as you're rising up and into the future. 10,

11, 12 the tunnel is now getting a little bit lighter and you can perceive a light at the end, another white light just like the white light that is surrounding you. 13, 14, 15 now you are almost there. Focus carefully. You can perceive a door in front of you to this left tunnel that you are in now. The door will be opened in just a few moments and you will see yourself in the future. The words "sleep now and rest" will always detach you from any scene you are experiencing and allow you to await further instructions. 16, 17 it's very bright now and you are putting your hands on the door. 18 you open the door. 19 you step into this future, to this future scene. 20 carefully focus on your surroundings, look around you, see what you perceive. Can you perceive yourself? Can you perceive other people around you? Focus on the environment. What does it look like? Carefully focus on this. Use complete objectivity. Block out any information from the past that might have interfered with the quality of the scene. Use only what your subconscious and superconscious mind level will observe. Now take a few moments, focus carefully on the scene, find out where you are, what you are doing, and why you are there. Take a few moments; let the scene manifest itself.

Play New Age music for 3 minutes.

Now focus very carefully on what year this is. Think for a moment. Numbers will appear before your inner eyes. You will have knowledge of the year that you are in right now. Carefully focus on this year and these numbers. They will appear before you. Use this as an example of other information that you are going to obtain. I want you to perceive this scene completely, carry it through to completion. I want you to perceive exactly where you are, the name, the date, the place, and other details.

I want you to carry these scenes to completion, and follow them through carefully for the next few moments. The scene will become clear and you will perceive the sequence of what exactly is happening to you.

Play New Age music for 3 minutes.

You've done very well. Now you are going to move to another event. I want you to focus on a difference in the same future time. Perceive what is going on and why this is important to you. Perceive the year, the environment, the presence of others. Let the information flow.

Play New Age music for 3 minutes.

As you perceive the details of the next scene, focus in on your purpose. Focus in on what you are learning and what you are unable to learn. Perceive any sequence of events that led up to this situation. Let the information flow surrounding this all-important future event now.

Play New Age music for 3 minutes.

You have done very well. Now I want you to rise to the superconscious mind level to evaluate this future experience and apply this knowledge to your current life and situations. 1 rising up. 2 rising higher. 3 halfway there. 4 almost there, 5 you are there. Let your higher self assist you in making the most out of this experience. Do this now.

Play New Age music for 3 minutes.

Label this frequency as number 1, 2, 3, 4, or 5, and separate it completely as you do this exercise again. If at any time you perceive an ideal frequency that you would like to be programmed to, just concentrate on that number. Do this now.

Play New Age music for 1 minute.

> All right now. Sleep now and rest. You have done very, very well. I'm going to count forward from 1 to 5. When I reach the count of 5, you will be able to remember everything you experienced. You'll feel very relaxed, refreshed, and able to do whatever you have planned for the rest of the day or evening. You'll feel very positive about what you've just experienced and very motivated about your confidence and ability to play this tape again to experience future frequencies. All right now. 1 very, very deep. 2 you're getting a little bit lighter. 3 you're getting much, much lighter. 4 very, very light. 5 awaken. Wide awake and refreshed.

This third exercise allows you to choose a specific date and location to visit. Precede this exercise by using a relaxation technique that works for you, or the hypnosis method I previously presented. When you have achieved a relaxed state, begin these steps:

1. Instruct yourself to travel to a specific date in the past or future. Along with this date, name a precise location to coincide with this date.

2. Say to yourself, "I am now about to embark on a voyage through time to (*state location*) in the year (*give date*). Intensely concentrate all of your attention on this place and date and actually visualize yourself moving to this specific destination.

It is helpful to select historical periods in the past to gain experience with this approach. Another helpful suggestion is to practice this technique just prior to falling asleep. This will effectively program your subconscious to initiate a dream exploration of this destination. Don't forget to tell yourself to recall this trip the following morning upon awakening.

A future life time travel experiment

In my first book, *Past Lives—Future Lives,* I presented a rather unusual future life progression. My patient, a woman named Kim, related a life in the twenty-second century in which she was Barbara, a member of a futuristic think tank, researching techniques to better humankind.

She worked in an underground complex with her mentor, Howard Pennington. Howard was the reincarnation of Kim's fiancé who died of leukemia before they could be married in her current life.

An interesting technological component of this complex was the small vehicles powered by air cushions. These cars moved by projecting an air current, creating a "whooshing" sound, and transporting Barbara and her co-workers through the complex. When I conducted a future life progression on NBC's *The Other Side,* a young woman who was unfamiliar with my work and who had no belief in reincarnation described a twenty-second-century future life in New York City as a lawyer. The mode of transportation she used was a car with no wheels that moved by this same air cushioning principle!

Barbara's project dealt with light refraction and ionization of molecular structure, with the eventual aim to alter the molecular structure of the brain in order to rid humankind of certain destructive tendencies.

The specific project in which Barbara was involved worked with a time biotelemetry concept. Several hundred years of time were condensed into a few hours in the laboratory through the use of advanced electronic gadgetry, in order for the subject to benefit from the entire spectrum of human emotions during this relatively brief span of time.

Past life regression was accomplished through this apparatus and a molecular ionization approach. Naturally, it was physically impossible for the subject to remember or comprehend this rapid scan of their previous incarnations. Reprogramming and emotional cleansing were their only concerns.

The problem was that this method just didn't seem to work as well as they hoped. Eventually they slowed down the procedure so that the subject could recall each past life they re-experienced. Throughout this chapter I summarized Barbara's past lives during the eighteenth century in France as a servant to a French nobleman, a male guard to the pope during the sixteenth century, a Chinese female over 1,000 years ago, and a male advisor to a Chinese emperor.

My explanation for their limited success was twofold. For one thing they didn't access the subject's future lives, and this limited any significant form of empowerment. Second, no energy cleansings or superconscious mind taps were conducted.

To experience your own future lifetime in reference to contact with time travelers or just to explore the centuries to come, try this self-hypnosis exercise:

Now listen very carefully. I want you to imagine a bright white light coming down from above and entering the top of your head, filling your entire body. See it, feel it, and it becomes reality. Now imagine an aura of pure white light emanating from your heart region, again surrounding your entire body. Protecting you. See it, feel it, and it becomes reality. Now only your masters and guides and highly evolved loving entities who mean you well will be able to influence you during this or any other hypnotic session. You are totally protected by this aura of pure white light. Focus carefully on my voice as your subconscious mind's memory bank has memories of all past, present, and future lifetimes. This tape will help guide you into the future, the future of another lifetime. I am going to be counting forward from 1 to 20. As I count forward from 1 to 20 you are going to imagine yourself moving through a tunnel. Near the end of this count you will perceive the tunnel divide and veer off to the left and to the right, the right representing the past, the left representing the future. You're going to veer to the left, through the left tunnel and this will take you into the future. On the count of 20 you will perceive yourself in the future. Your subconscious and superconscious mind levels have all the knowledge and information that you desire. Carefully and comfortably feel yourself moving into the future with each count from one to twenty. Listen carefully now. Number 1 feel yourself now moving forward to the future, into this very, very deep, dark tunnel. 2, 3 further and further into the future.

4, 5, 6 the tunnel is very, very dark. It is a little bit disorienting but you know you're moving into the future. 7, 8, 9 it's more stable now and you feel comfortable, you feel almost as if you're floating, as you're rising up and into the future. 10, 11, 12 the tunnel is now getting a little bit lighter and you can perceive a light at the end, another white light just like the white light that is surrounding you.

13, 14, 15. Now you are almost there. Focus carefully. You can perceive a door in front of you to the left of the tunnel that you are in right now. The door will be opened in just a few moments and you will see yourself in the future. The words "sleep now and rest" will always detach you from any scene you are experiencing and allow you to await further instructions. 16, 17. It's very bright now and you are putting your hands on the door. 18 you open the door, 19 you step into this future, to this future scene. Number 20. Carefully focus on your surroundings, look around you, see what you perceive. Can you perceive yourself? Can you perceive other people around you? Focus on the environment. What does it look like? Carefully focus on this. Use your complete objectivity. Block out any information from the past that might have interfered with the quality of the scene. Use only what your subconscious and superconscious mind level will observe. Now take a few moments, focus carefully on the scene, find out where you are, what you are doing, why you are there. Take a few moments, let the scene manifest itself.

Play New Age music for 3 minutes.

Now focus very carefully on what year this is. Think for a moment. Numbers will appear before your inner eyes. You will have knowledge of the year that you are in right now. Carefully focus on this year and these numbers. They will appear before you. Use this as an example of other information that you are going to obtain. I want you to perceive exactly where you are, who you are, the name, the date, the place. I want you to carry these scenes to completion, follow them through carefully for the next few moments. The scene will become clear and you will perceive the sequence of what exactly is happening to you.

Play New Age music for 3 minutes.

You've done very well. Now you are going to move to another event. I want you to focus on a different experience in the same future time. Perceive what is going on and why this is important to you. Perceive the year, the environment, the presence of others. Let the information flow.

Play New Age music for 3 minutes.

As you perceive the details of the next scene, focus also on your purpose—your purpose in this future time and how it is affecting your karmic subcycle. Focus in on what you are learning, what you are able to learn. Perceive any sequence of events that led up to this situation. If you have any contact whatsoever with time travelers, let the information flow surrounding this all important future event now.

Play New Age music for 3 minutes.

Sleep now and rest. You've done very well. Now I want you to rise to the superconscious mind level to evaluate this future experience and apply this knowledge to your current life and situations. 1, rising up, 2 rising higher, 3 halfway there, 4 almost there, number 5—you are there. Let your masters and guides assist you in making the most out of this experience. Do this now.

Play New Age music for 3 minutes.

All right now. Sleep now and rest. You did very very well. Listen very carefully. I'm going to count backward now from 5 to 1. This time when I reach 1 you will be back in the present, you will be able to remember everything you experienced and re-experienced you'll feel very relaxed and refreshed, you'll be able to do whatever you have planned for the rest of the day or evening. You'll feel very positive about what you've just experienced and very motivated about your confidence and ability to play this tape again to experience additional future events. All right now. 5 moving back in time, 4 move farther back, 3 halfway there, 2 almost there, number 1 you are back in the present. I'm gong to count forward from 1 to 5 and when I reach the count of 5 you will be wide awake, relaxed, and refreshed. Number 1 very, very deep. Number 2 you are getting a little bit lighter. Number 3 halfway there. Number 4 very, very light. Number 5 awaken.

We must understand that according to quantum mechanics, we are much more than external observers of the universe. We cannot separate ourselves from the very events that we are observing, and these observations determine the final outcome of the events themselves. It is our consciousness that defines the past, present, and future—not the universe. There is thus no violation of causality in traveling back, sideways, or forward in time. We, in effect, create our own reality through the use of our mind. Our minds are time machines and are capable of traveling into the past, future, and parallel time periods to give meaning to our existence on this planet and, if used properly, to psychically empower us to achieve our true karmic purpose. This higher form of quantum reality is necessary to us in achieving our destiny through the tunnel of time.

Why some progressions come true while others don't

As I previously discussed, there are five main frequencies for the future, as well as the past. We are at every moment transmitting quantum waves into the "futures" based on our soul's frequency vibrational rate. The higher our soul's rate, the more desirable our future options become. This is why I highly recommend superconscious mind taps to effect cleansing.

At the same time the yous and mes in these future parallel universes are sending back through time quantum waves which interact with the waves produced in our present.

There are now two possible outcomes. A match of these two quantum waves may create a strong combined wave, resulting in a meaningful resonance to us that effectively creates a real future from our current perspective and a real memory of sequences from the viewpoint of this future frequency. Any data we receive from the future, such as a career choice, lottery number, etc., will come true for us at the indicated time and date.

The second possibility is that these two quantum waves do not match. Now this modulation creates a wave of such weak strength that there is no resonance. Consequently, the meaning (probability) of this future frequency is too low for it to become a part of our current reality. Most of the data received from this future parallel universe will not occur in our current world. I say most, because in the near future many frameworks of the future paths are identical. They tend to branch off in different outcomes as you move farther forward in time.

Visionaries, psychics, and highly intuitive and creative people are simply successfully marrying these two quantum waves and increasing the possibility of this future frequency occurring. The stronger the combined quantum wave, the greater the probability (and more meaningful) of this path occurring to us now.

From a spiritual growth perspective, the more we resonate our present/future quantum waves, the more we live in a timeless state, or true state of reality. The result is a highly evolved, empowered and greatly fulfilling life. Failure to do this creates a time-bound dysfunctional and disconnected lifestyle, unfortunately characteristic of most people lost in their karmic subcycles.

The inability to discriminate these future quantum waves effectively may very well explain psychiatric illness such as schizophrenia and multiple personality disorders, UFO abductions, spontaneous human combustion and unexplained anomalies such as the discovery of human footprints along with dinosaur tracks in the Paluxy River near Glen Rose, Texas or the thousands of fish that fell from the sky in an 1860 thunderstorm in the city of Singapore.

Fifth dimension travel

This exercise represents the culmination of the various hypnotic techniques in reference to the theme of this book. When you practice this script, several different types of experiences are available to you. First, you will be guided to merge with your Higher Self, enter a blackhole, and explore the fifth dimension. Next, you will be presented with the opportunity to communicate with a time traveler who has worked with you in the past, or previous lives. Third, you will be guided into one of your own parallel selves. This is a completely different body on the Earth planet that a component of your soul is occupying. In other words, both you and this individual's soul can trace your respective soul's energy back to a common oversoul. Finally, this method allows you to explore any aspect of the past, future, or parallel universes by exiting through a whitehole. You will be safely guided back to your present location and body at the end of this voyage. As with all of my self-hypnotic techniques, this is perfectly safe.

> Now listen very carefully. I want you to imagine a bright white light coming down from above and entering the top of your head, filling your entire body. See it, feel it, and it becomes reality. Now imagine an aura of pure white light emanating

from your heart region. Again, surrounding your entire body, protecting you. See it, feel it, and it becomes reality. Now only your Higher Self, Masters and Guides, and highly evolved loving entities who mean you well will be able to influence you during this or any other hypnotic session. You are totally protected by this aura of pure white light. In a few moments I am going to count from 1 to 20. As I do so, you will feel yourself rising up to the superconscious mind level where you will be able to communicate with your Higher Self. Number 1 rising up. 2, 3, 4 rising higher. 5, 6, 7 letting information flow. 8, 9, 10 you are halfway there. 11, 12, 13 feel yourself rising even higher. 14, 15, 16 almost there. 17, 18, 19 number 20 you are there. Take a moment and orient yourself to the superconscious mind level. Now I want you to merge with your Higher Self and be prepared to enter a blackhole. Take a few moments and perceive yourself actually entering and merging with the white light of your Higher Self. Do this now.

Play New Age music for 2 minutes.

Now that you have become one with your Higher Self, you are free to control this experience, completely protected and out of your body. See a blackhole in front of you and enter it. This is a gateway into the Fifth Dimension. From here you can travel to parallel universes, the past, the future, or just remain in this Fifth Dimension hyperspace. Focus on meeting other souls in this hyper-universe. Take a few moments and open yourself to encountering other entities. You are perfectly safe and protected, and you will only attract positive people and souls into your awareness. Do this now.

Play New Age music for 3 minutes.

You have done very well. At this time I would like you to attract a time traveler from our future who has worked with you in the past or previous lifetimes. You will be able to communicate with this time traveler by telepathy. Do this now.

Play New Age music for 4 minutes.

Very good. At this time I want you to specifically explore one of your own parallel selves. This is another human on the Earth plane whose soul and yours may be traced back to a common oversoul ancestor. Travel through the Fifth Dimension now and explore another existence that a part of your current soul shares today on the Earth plane in another body. Do this now.

Play New Age music for 3 minutes.

All right, you have done very well. In just a few moments I am going to count up from 1 to 5. When I reach the count of 5 you will be back in hyperspace from where you began this voyage. 1 you are returning to hyperspace, 2 moving closer, 3 halfway there, 4 almost there, and 5 you are there. I'm going to count forward from 1 to 5. When I reach the count of 5 you will be back in your physical body in the present, you will be able to remember everything you experienced and re-experienced. You'll feel very relaxed, refreshed, and able to do whatever you have planned for the rest of the day or evening. You'll feel very positive about what you've just experienced and very motivated about your confidence and ability to play this tape again to experience the Fifth Dimension. All right now. 1 very, very deep, 2 you're getting a little bit lighter, 3 you're getting much, much lighter, 4 very, very light, 5 awaken. Wide awake and refreshed.

Chapter 10

Evidence of time travelers

I n this chapter we will discuss evidence discovered that appears out of date with current archaeology and paleontology. Certain objects have been carbon dated to prove that they existed hundreds of thousands to billions of years before human beings had the capability of creating them.

For some, these findings are evidence of advanced civilizations on this planet well before our current paradigms. Others assign extraterrestrial visitations to our planet as their origin. The time travelers have telepathically communicated to my patients the fact that these items were brought from various periods of our history to the distant past as a result of three factors.

- They were transported back in time as part of experiments with hyperspace and wormholes.

- These items were purposely brought back into our distant past by futuristic chrononauts, after making several stops in other time periods, for the purpose of stimulating our minds to figure this out for ourself and speed up our intellectual evolution.
- Some of these were originally collected from other planets, but were placed back in time by our chrononauts.

My source for this section is *Forbidden Archeology: The Hidden History of the Human Race* by Michael Cremo and Richard L. Thompson. Consider the following finds:

- A North Britain nail embedded in a block of sandstone from the Kingoddie Quarry dated from 360 to 408 million years ago and discovered in 1844.
- Also in 1844, a gold thread embedded in a stone found eight feet beneath the ground originated from 320 to 360 million years ago.
- A metallic vase with beautifully inlaid figures, found in Dorchester, Massachusetts, dated back some 600 million years ago.
- A chalk ball found 246 feet below the ground in Laon, France, in 1861 is forty-five to fifty-five million years old.
- In 1871 a coinlike object was discovered in a well near Lawn Ridge, Illinois. This was carbondated to between 200,000 to 400,000 years old. The coin was polygonal (nearly circular) in shape with crudely produced figures and glyph-like inscriptions on both sides in a language currently unknown. It has been determined that this coin must have been made in a machine shop. Records show the first such coins in use by humans were made in Asia Minor during the eighth century B.C.
- A clay figurine was found at Nampa, Idaho, in 1889; it dated to about two million years ago.
- A partial sole from a shoe was uncovered in 1922 in Nevada. This item is from 213 to 248 million years old.
- A metallic sphere was found in South Africa that contains three parallel grooves around its equator. It is *not* a naturally produced piece of ore. Although it is obviously manmade, it dates back to 2.8 *billion* years ago.

These spheres are limonite, which is a type of iron ore. Hundreds of these have been discovered, and are so hard that they cannot be scratched with a steel point. Although limonite occurs naturally in clusters, it does not appear in isolated, perfectly round stones, or with parallel grooves encircling them. The only life that existed 2.8 billion years ago was bacteria and primitive plants.[1]

Animal mutilations

An interesting observation regarding DNA is made by geneticists. There is only one genetic code for terrestrial life. Many biologists believe that land animals arose from "primeval soup," but if that were accurate, several different genetic codes should exist. Perhaps this serves to support a premeditative artificial genetic manipulation of life on our planet by the time travelers in order to produce us.

When we add this to the many unexplained living and dead animals that have fallen from the sky, we have additional evidence of chrononauts. These animals have included frogs, fish, insects, worms, reptiles, crabs, and snails. One hypothesis for this occurrence is that they were dumped from tanks aboard time traveler crafts after their research value ended.

The mutilations of sheep, horses, cattle, and hogs in America and abroad further adds to genetic research by time travelers. UFO sightings have been linked to these mutilations, despite attempts of government coverup.

Especially interesting about these animal mutilations are the following observations:

- Skillful surgical incisions are made with instruments that leave burn marks on the bodies.

- The bodies are avoided by predators.

- These animals are found many miles from their pastures, some in inaccessible mountainous areas.

---

1   M. A Cremo and R. L. Thompson, *Forbidden Archeology: The Hidden History of the Human Race* (Los Angeles: Bhaktivedanta Book Pub., Inc., 1993).

- Some carcasses have no blood left.

- Even when there is snow on the ground or it's muddy, no tracks are found.

Dr. Richard Neal, Jr. is a gynecologist who for over twenty years has examined many abductees. He conducted a study surveying common areas of manipulation on abductees and reported the following:

> The nasal cavity, ears, eyes and genitalia appear to be the physical areas of greatest interest to abducting aliens. The umbilical region (navel) is as well, but in females only.
>
> Many abductees have described a thin probe with a tiny ball on its end being inserted into the nostril—usually on the right side. They are able to hear a "crushing" type sound as the bone in this area is apparently being penetrated. Many will have nosebleeds following these examinations….Many researchers believe that alien technology is being used to insert an implant into this area for future tracking of the individual….Documented evidence has also shown that some abductees have been probed in their eyes and ears with a similar instrument. With eyes being involved, abductees may experience temporary blindness, blurred vision, swollen, watery, and painful eyes (photophtalmia), acute conjunctivitis (red and irritated, inflamed eyes called "pink eye" in lay terms).

In reference to the scars reported by abductees, Dr. Neal states they fall into two basic groups:

- A thin, straight, hairline cut, linear, about 1 to 3 inches long, and

- A circular or scoop-like depression, about ⅛ inch to ¾ inch in diameter and maybe as much as ¼ inch deep.[2]

---

2   R. Neal, M.D., "Generations of Abductions: A Medical Casebook," *UFO Magazine,* 3 (2) (1988), p. 22.

The Sumerian experiment

We have many ancient records of some type of advanced being interacting with our civilizations. For example, Carl Sagan and I. S. Shklovskii cite a Sumerian legend:

> Taken at face value the legend suggests that contact occurred between human beings and a nonhuman civilization of immense powers on the shores of the Persian Gulf, perhaps near the site of the ancient city of Eridu, and in the fourth millennium B.C. or earlier.[3]
>
> An advanced being used to converse with men. . . . He gave them an insight into letters and sciences and every kind of art. He taught them how to construct houses, to found temples, to compile laws, and explained to them the principles of geometrical knowledge. He made them distinguish the seeds of the earth and showed them how to collect fruits. In short, he instructed them in everything which could tend to humanize mankind.[4]

Another interesting aspect of the Sumerian (3,000 B.C.) city Eridu is that it may have been our first civilization. Eridu is known as the Babylonian Eden. Babylon followed the Sumerian culture, and the legend describing a man named Adapa is so much like Genesis that Adapa is called the Babylonian Adam. The Babylonian inscription refers to him as: "Adapa, the seed of Mankind" and "Adapa, the wise man of Eridu." Was Adapa a time traveler?

The Sumerians developed *cuneiform* writing and one of its cities, Ur, was the birthplace of the Hebrew Abraham. This civilization was conquered by the Akkadians, Amorites, and Persians and their cuneiform writing, originally pictographic and later wedge-shaped imprints, was replaced by the North Semite script of Aramaic languages.

---

3   Carl Sagan and I. S. Shklovskii, *Intelligent Life in the Universe* (San Francisco: Holden-Day, Inc., 1966), p. 456.

4   Ibid., p. 457.

The Piri Reis maps

A very interesting unexplained phenomenon that has boggled the human mind for years is the Piri Reis maps. The time travelers have described their taking Piri Reis on board their crafts to guide his map-making accuracy. The story of the Piri Reis map would make a book in itself.

In 1929 in the Seray Library in Constantinople (Istanbul today) a map traced on a parchment was discovered that was dated the month of Nuharrem in the year 919 of the Prophet (A.D. 1513). It was signed by Piri Ibn Haji Memmed, the complete name of Admiral Piri Reis.

Piri Reis was the nephew of the famous pirate Kemal Reis, and he took part in several pirate expeditions. He was eventually appointed governor of Egypt. In Cairo in A.D. 1554 this pirate was beheaded for his nefarious activities.

The maps drawn by Piri Reis described his many voyages around the world. Those found in the Seray Library quite accurately depicted both coasts of the Atlantic ocean and a clear representation of America. Christopher Columbus reportedly used Reis' maps.

One specific map drawn by Piri Reis that drew international attention was that of Antarctica. American engineer, mathematician, and researcher Arlington Mallery proved mathematically that this map required advance knowledge of spherical trigonometry. It also dated from a period preceding the era when ice covered the Queen Maud Land region of Antarctica. In other words, this map originated well before 1513!

Professor Charles H. Hapgood of Keene State College in New Hampshire proved that this map required the use of an aircraft, was a copy of a map that was older than any we possess, probably originating around 15,000 B.C., and was constructed by people who knew about the Earth's curvature and spherical trigonometry. These were, of course, the time travelers.

We find the gulf of Venezuela, the Amazon River, and Antarctica on this puzzling map. Antarctica wasn't discovered until 1818! What is most striking is that the Piri Reis map had to have come from a source that existed prior to the ice covering the Queen Maud Land region of Antarctica, since it accurately portrays the borders that have been covered by ice for at least 15,000 years.

Other maps such as the Camerio Renaissance map dated 1502, a Venetian map from 1484, and an engraved stone in China dated A.D. 1137 illustrated the same grid as found on the Piri Reis map. They obviously originated from the same source as the time travelers.

As an aside, there was one reference in my records of a patient reporting to me that the time travelers influenced the Mayan civilization. I am not surprised by that fact at all. Consider the fact that the Mayan year lasted 365.2420 days. Most modern calculations compute a year to be 365.2423 days.

The Mayans determined the length of the moon's cycle to within four-thousandths of a day, in addition to being accurate to the extent of one ten-thousandth of a day for an Earth year.

Sadly, we can only account for about five percent of the documents and other records from the past 3,000 years. In 146 B.C. the Romans burned a library of 500,000 volumes in Carthage. The Alexandrian Library in Egypt (the greatest loss from antiquity) was lost through fires and invasions, the last during the Arab conquest in the seventh century A.D. Also disappearing without a trace was the massive library of the Russian Tsar, Ivan the Terrible.

Was this due to the time traveler's concern for the preservation of certain secrets, or just acts of nature and human ignorance? These time travelers did leave us specific clues to stimulate our own intelligence to discover their existence.

Masonry—a legacy of the time travelers

The idea that Freemasonry originated in ancient Egypt was proposed by the eighteenth-century Italian adventurer Conte di Alessandro Cagliostro (1743–1795), whose real name was Giuseppe Balsamo. Cagliostro gained fame in Paris for his skills in alchemy and magic, but was arrested for promoting Freemasonry and died in prison in Italy.

Cagliostro developed the rite known as "Egyptian Masonry." The purpose of this order was to initiate its members into all the secrets of the priests of ancient Egypt. The time travelers clearly stated that they used Masonry to educate us in all aspects of life, and to instruct us in the secrets of the universe. These chrononauts identified the Mystery Schools as their invention, in order to accomplish these goals since ancient times.

When Cagliostro founded his society very little was known about ancient Egypt. No one could understand even the simplest of hieroglyphics, and what little scholars knew about Egyptian religion and cultures came from often-inaccurate Greek and Latin writings. It was when Cagliostro attempted to establish a branch of Egyptian Masonry in Rome that he met the opposition of the Catholic Church to freemasonry. He was arrested by the Inquisition and later died in prison.

R. A. Schwaller de Lubicz was an orientalist and philosopher who made a long and detailed study of Egyptian monuments, especially the Temple of Luxor. De Lubicz, who died in 1960, advocated a theory that Egypt was an advanced culture in which science, religion, philosophy, and art were all parts of a unified system of knowledge that belonged to a secret society called "The Temple." The task of the Temple was to direct the cultural and artistic life of the country, and encompass its knowledge of cosmic laws in the art and architecture of Egypt.

De Lubicz believed that Egyptians did not use literal meanings for their hieroglyphics, but symbolic ones. If hieroglyphic writings are interpreted in the light of symbolism, and if the modern reader tries to think like an ancient Egyptian, then such writings become rich with significance, conveying an organic view of man and the universe in which he lives as interdependent parts making up a greater whole.

When Egyptian priests dedicated a temple to a particular god, they were not celebrating the wealth or political importance of the priests of that god. They were expressing, in the language of architectural symbolism, the spiritual laws relating to the specific cosmic functions that the god symbolized. The origin of the universe, according to the ancient Egyptians, was viewed as a movement from unity to multiplicity, from the one to the many. This concept resembles the theories of many modern physicists who believe that the universe as we know it originated in a "big bang."

It was impossible for man to understand directly what happened at the creation of the universe, but he could arrive at a symbolic understanding of it through myth, through the architecture of temples and monuments, and through self-understanding, according to these ancients.

The Egyptians, inspired by the time travelers, looked upon man as a divine creation whose physical and spiritual qualities contained every one of the cosmic laws.

As I discuss Freemasonry, my main source of information is Albert Pike's classic book, *Morals and Dogma of the Ancient and Accepted Scottish Rite of Freemasonry.*[5] Public religious worship in most of the ancient nations was not the only worship of those who were initiated into the Mysteries. Their real worship was in the Mysteries, from which the masses were excluded. This degree is equivalent in Masonry to the Lesser Mysteries into which all were initiated. Only a few were initiated into the Greater Mysteries.

In the beginning, the time travelers created a fairly simple system for the Mysteries in instructing ancient man about the truths concerning morality and religion. It was ancient man that distorted this system and complicated the paradigm. This was done to significantly restrict the number of adepts who could enter the higher degrees.

The beginnings of Masonry in ancient times unfortunately represented another failed experiment of the time travelers, but it is among their greatest legacies. One of the chief goals of Masonry through the centuries has been spiritually motivated action aimed at easing the existing suffering of those around them and of changing the circumstances under which they lived so as to guarantee future betterment.

---

5 A. Pike, *Morals and Dogma of the Ancient and Accepted Scottish Right of Freemasonry* (Charleston, South Carolina: A.M. 5632, 1950).

Since, as we have seen with Cagliostro, the Masons were persecuted throughout history, each generation of Masons had to adapt in the best way possible to fit the social and political circumstances around them—hence the development of signs, symbols, and secret physical acts and words that only fellow Masons could understand. Although Masons deny the existence of secrets, the ritual threatens more severe punishment for the betrayal of secrets than for anything else. Betrayal of secrets in the earlier days supposedly extracted a death sentence. This was not what the time travelers had in mind. Like most of their experiments, this one took on a life of its own.

The medieval phase of Masonry was called Operative Masonry, since these guild members functioned as highly trained construction workers and master builders. Later on the Speculative Masonry orders were established as a social fraternity of men based on the precepts and examples of those former guild workers. The once-severe penalties for revealing secrets have been scaled down considerably today.

These Speculative Masons carried on one of the earlier ancient traditions of thinking and meditation about life, hence the term "speculative." Speculative Masons are supposed to be builders too—builders of character and the inner man, called the human "Temple of God." There are no nobler precepts and principles anywhere than those taught in the initiation ceremonies of the various degrees of Masonry.

Historically, the first three degrees of Masons represent the same three degrees recognized by the operative Mason in the building of King Solomon's Temple. The wise and virtuous Hiram, the master builder in charge of construction of King Solomon's temple in the ancient land of the Jews, was murdered. Hiram's death was to be remembered—by order from King Solomon—at a special ceremony each year. The Fifth Degree ceremony is a reenactment of Hiram's funeral ceremony which Solomon and King Hiram of Tyre both attend.

As was the case with ancient Egyptian hieroglyphics, Masonry is rich with allegory and symbolism. Masonry denies being a religion, but it claims to live and teach the fundamental truths of all faiths. Morality and righteous living are claimed to be the foundation of Masonry.

Masonry claims credit for the teaching and living of every good principle in any and all religions, philosophies, and political aspects of life. Masonry encompasses the whole of life—education, morality, nobility, religion, politics, dedication to home, family, neighbor, community, state, nation, and the world, as well as every worthy precept, principle, or ideal that humankind has ever represented.

To illustrate Masonry's tie to the Mysteries, consider the Knight of the Brazen Serpent or Twenty-fifth Degree. In the initiation the candidate is passed through the House of the Earth, the House of the Planets, the House of the Sun and Moon, and on to the House of the Light. In each House he is to learn more and be tested to determine his understanding and constancy. Continual education is always emphasized.

Four main topics are discussed within this degree of Masonry. These subjects are the soul, the heavens, the serpent, and symbolism. Ancient Egyptians considered the serpent when extended full length a symbol of divine wisdom. With its tail in its mouth, forming a circle, it symbolized Eternity. Unfortunately, modern Masons copied the ancients' tendency to teach their "sacred truths of the universe" to a select few.

According to the ancients, the mysteries of the True original religion that God gave to man was inexpressible in human terms. Symbolism was the mechanism used to convert a revealed truth to a hidden one. Only those initiates who understood this symbolism were allowed to learn it. The Mystic Ladder has seven rungs. These are: justice, a benign nature, faith, kindness, victory and glory, patience, and understanding or intelligence. The esoteric significance of the ladder is for the initiated only—"esoteric" means something designed for and understood only by the initiated.

One aspect of spiritual growth that the time travelers failed to achieve with us concerns a word that supposedly signified the reality of the Creator's Omnipotent Power. The word was lost because it was ineffable and never spoken until it was forgotten. If it could be recovered, its possessors would have special powers not possessed by anyone else. They failed to recover that lost word and so have Masons and the time travelers failed.

A success that has affected the political course of history deals with the Masons' devotion to democracy, freedom of speech, and patriotism. In past times the Masonic lodges existed in countries that suppressed free thought, speech, and action. That meant that free-thinking, independent workmen were inviting trouble if they tried to advance their democratic philosophies.

The determination and struggles of the Masons throughout history resulted in the religious and political freedom that exists in the world today. Early American Masons, like George Washington, Benjamin Franklin, and others, were familiar only with the simple requirements taught in the initiation and the basic democratic goals of this group. Many other presidents of the United States have been Masons. America has been more responsible for the spread of Masonic philosophies of democracy than any other nation.

Stonehenge

Located in Salisbury, England, about eighty miles west of London, are a number of giant standing stones, some in pairs with lintel stones across their tops, and also many fallen stones. Stonehenge was not built by the Druids, as was sometimes supposed, but at an earlier time under the strict supervision of the time travelers. All the archeological evidence makes it clear that the structure had existed for over 1,000 years before the arrival of Druidic cults in Britain. Just as we note in other megalithic structures such as Carnac in northwest France, Stonehenge was designed as an astronomical observatory. We have already mentioned that it lies in a ley line in Chapter 7.

The Moon deviates from its regular course by an almost imperceptible amount—0.9 degrees over a long period. Yet when astronomer G. S. Hawkins studied the methods of observation used by the builders of Stonehenge, he discovered that this minute deviation of 0.9 degrees had been recognized more than 3,000 years ago. It was not discovered by modern astronomers until the sixteenth century! Hawkins feels

Stonehenge is a prehistoric computer.[6] The stone standing alone to the northeast of the main structure is called the Heel Stone, derived from the Anglo-Saxon *helan*, to hide—but no one knows what it hides. Does this remind you of the Mystery Schools? At the summer solstice the Sun rises directly over the Heel Stone as seen from the center of Stonehenge.

Nobody denies that sites such as Stonehenge were used for religious observances. Many modern churches are constructed so that the window behind the altar catches the light of the rising Sun; but that is purely a question of dramatic effect. It would certainly cause comment if we installed computers behind the altars of our cathedrals, or used the towers to house astronomical telescopes. A sacred place like Stonehenge would reach a maximum intensity at periods when the influence of the heavenly bodies of the Earth's forces were strongest. These would be the obvious times for major religious rites.

We cannot ascribe Stonehenge to the Druids or Romans, since it was built long before these civilizations existed. In addition, there is no mention of the Druids' architectural skills. They may have been astronomers, but they certainly were not technically capable of hoisting huge stones weighing as much as twelve tons each above a pair of upright stones, and lowering them into place with enough precision that the mortised notches on the undersides of the capstones hooked over the stone tenons atop the uprights.

The setting of Stonehenge stones surrounded by a circular earthwork is only a shell of what it once was. About half of the original stones are gone. Many others lie toppled and broken.

Stonehenge consists of two concentric rings of upright stones enclosing a pair of horseshoe-shaped stone forms. Completing the complex are several solitary stones, including the Slaughter Stone and Heel Stone. A shallow ditch at its northeastern rim connects Stonehenge with the Avon River, about a mile and a half away.

---

6   G. S. Hawkins, *Stonehenge Decoded* (New York: Dell, 1966).

This megalith is constructed primarily of bluestone, a type of blue-tinted dolerite, and sarsen, a variety of sandstone harder than granite. The bluestones have been traced to a Welsh quarry about 130 miles northwest of Salisbury Plain; the sarsen slabs were brought from the Marlborough Downs, about twenty miles north of the site. Wheeled vehicles were unknown in Britain during the time of Stonehenge's construction. We have seen in Roger's past life (chapter 4) how the time traveler's anti-gravity flying vehicles could have accomplished this task.

Officially, the builders of Stonehenge have not been identified, nor has the purpose of this structure ever been firmly established. We find about 50,000 megaliths around the world, mostly in western Europe and North Africa. The legacy of Stonehenge is similar to that of the pyramids at Giza, the Mayan pyramids, and others. They represent evidence of time travelers assisting our development in ancient times.

Humanity as evidence

Anthropologists and archaeologists are quick to point out the slowness of evolution. Our predecessor is usually accepted to be Cro-Magnon man, who came onto the scene approximately 40,000 B.C. He evolved from Neanderthal man, a much less intelligent human.

Evolution just doesn't work that fast. Most mutations do not survive long in nature. From skeletal remains and cave paintings in places like Lascaux, France, we may say that physically and possibly intellectually this upstart species of Cro-Magnon man was very close to us in potential.

I described how the time travelers sped up our evolution at the same time that they arranged to rid our planet of the dinosaurs. Through the past sixty-five million years these chrononauts have been our guardian angels and genetic surgeons. This may sound like a radical and unscientific theory, but no conventional explanation satisfactorily explains our emergence and technological achievements.

Consider another theory in relationship to our evolution from African apes. The conventional paradigm is that our genetic predecessor was a small ape called *Australopithecus africans* in Lake Victoria about 800,000 years ago. A much larger ape, *Australopithecus robustus*, kicked us out of the jungle and we had to adapt to life on the Savannah.

Now let us discuss the aquatic ape theory. Many of our traits, such as a descended larynx, subcutaneous fat, and large brains, occur in sea mammals and not in the land primates that are more closely related to us. Walking upright and having sex face-to-face is not characteristic of other land mammals, but it is noted in chimpanzees living in swamps.

One conclusion from these facts is that our species evolved from a semi-aquatic environment, and not from a jungle to savannah transition. We can also point to the brain nutrients found in seafood that are much scarcer on land. This may have contributed to our increased brain size and functioning.

In ancient writings we find many examples of wise gods associated with the sea. The Babylonian god Oannes is an excellent example. This half man, half fish came from the sea and instructed terrestrial man in the arts of civilization. We can also point to the many mermaid legends.

The dolphin is considered second only to man in intelligence. This aquatic mammal has a very spiritual association and has been reported to both detect and treat human illnesses, such as autism. We note many ancient stories of benign contact between intelligent sea creatures and humans throughout the world.[7]

One reason I included the aquatic ape theory in this chapter relates to an expression one of the time travelers used in a telepathic communication with a young female waitress during her abduction. She asked this white-robed human chrononaut where our species came from, and he stated, "From the sea."

She assumed he was referring to classic evolution from marine life, and asked the time traveler for verification of this fact. He simply looked at her and smiled. The next telepathic communication was quite clear.

---

7   A. Cochrane and K. Callen, *Dolphins and their Power to Heal* (Santa Monica, CA: Healing Arts Press, 1992).

He said, "Your predecessors lived by and in the sea. They did not swing from trees and live off bananas. They made the water their home."

So it appears the aquatic ape theory is alive and well. All of those metaphysical associations with dolphins may have a strong scientific basis after all. If we did indeed evolve from aquatic apes, then the dolphins would have been long-time associates with our genetic and probably spiritual growth.

Conclusion

The Industrial Revolution was ushered in when Isaac Newton discovered and translated the classical laws of gravity into the theory of mechanics. James Maxwell gave us the fundamental laws of electromagnetic force in the mid-1860s, and brought electricity into our scientific stable. This resulted in such conveniences as radio, television, the telephone, household appliances, the dynamo, microwaves, lasers, computers, and a host of other amenities.

We harnessed nuclear energy in the mid-1940s and developed the atomic and hydrogen bombs. Nuclear energy also resulted in positive uses of this immense form of power. The possibility of finally understanding all of the cosmic forces that comprise our universe, whether it be through the superstring theory or something else, may actually allow us to empower ourselves beyond our wildest dreams.

Becoming the master of hyperspace should not deter us from our true purpose. That purpose is to grow spiritually and perfect our soul. In that regard the time travelers have so far failed.

Let us not forget that these chrononauts still abduct our citizens to study us, assist in their own fertility problems and educate us spiritually. By mastering hyperspace, they could be among us as you read this book. Their more rapid vibratory rate would make them invisible to our eyes, although they could see us and interact with our soul's energy, at least psychically.

It is rather difficult for the average person to envision ten or twenty-six dimensions. Just as our eyes are unable to see colors that are beyond our limited visual spectrum, what would we observe if our eyes could be made sensitive to radiations of longer wavelength than violet? We would see new colors that do not at present exist for us. If such new colors are a known possibility, why couldn't there be new dimensions?

Are the laws of nature actually violated by time travelers? I have already demonstrated that the works of Wheeler, Aharonov, D'Amato, and Albert clearly show that no violation of causality occurs as a result of time travel. Putting that aside, consider the fact that we simply do not know enough about the true nature and structure of reality to be in a position to make that assessment.

To conclude that something is "impossible" just because we have not sufficiently explored all aspects of the universe, with a *complete* understanding of its many components, is to make an unqualified judgment.

We need to reassess this paradigm of time travel, hyperspace, and hyper-universes with an open mind in order to truly embrace a balanced vision of human potential and spiritual growth. This is not a war between mainstream science and metaphysics or materialism versus occult ideology. It is quite simply a new and exciting path to ascension. Isn't that what life is all about?

Stephen Hawking, the Cambridge University theoretical physicist, states in his international bestseller, *A Brief History of Time:*

> The laws of science do not distinguish between the forward and backward direction of time....The progress of the human race

in understanding the universe has established a small corner of order in an increasingly disordered universe.[1]

Breaches in the fabric of space-time, whether created purposely by the time travelers or as a result of their failed experiments, could have unusual consequences for anyone who happened to become caught in them. Like the Vaughan children's disappearance, the teleportation of the Spanish soldier from Manila, or Benjamin Bathurst's unexplained vanishing nearly 200 years ago, something is occurring in our world that defies conventional explanation.

The ancient Chinese believed that the Earth is covered with lines of magnetic force, which they called *lung-mei,* or dragon paths. They believed that these paths extend over the entire world. Points at which several of the paths meet are "holy centers" invested with particular power, and are frequently marked by mountains, hills, and stone circles. We have seen the amazing ability of Stonehenge rocks to function like a primitive computer.

In more recent times ley lines have been proposed to explain some of these unusual occurrences in our world. The time travelers have for thousands of years been instructing us how to maximize the natural forces that comprise our realm.

Time travelers or aliens?

What we are dealing with in respect to our species development is a combination of extraterrestrial involvement (the insect alien and hybrid time travelers) along with our own species in the future returning to our time.

Consider the fact that Arthur C. Clarke predicts that we will make manned flights to Mars by the year 2005, build space cities by 2010, have a manned base on Mars in 2020 and explore our solar system by 2030.[2]

---

1   S. Hawking, *A Brief History of Time* (New York: Bantam Books, 1988), p. 152.
2   A. C. Clarke, *1984: Spring—A Choice of Futures* (New York: Ballantine, 1984), pp. 147, 148.

James Oberg of the NASA Space Center in Houston, Texas, discusses our potential for reshaping other planets to conform to our needs, something he calls *terraforming*. For example, future planetary engineering will include the following:

- Create an Earth-like atmosphere on the Moon.
- Use the hydrogen from the outer planets (Pluto, Uranus, Neptune) for rocket fuel and their rocky structure to create new habitable planets.
- Create a livable atmosphere on Venus by evaporating its clouds and cooling it.
- Establish rainfall on Mars to allow life to exist once again.[3]

From these projections we can see how possible it is for beings from other planets that are millions of years older than Earth to have established contact with us throughout our species history. From an evolutionary standpoint, the most advanced organism on our planet just one billion years ago was the worm. Maybe these ancient extraterrestrials were the original time travelers?

Our evolution began rather slowly—sexual reproduction has only been possible during the past 600 million years of our planet's five-billion-year history. Suddenly, we see an acceleration in evolution, no doubt brought on by time travelers working in concert with extraterrestrials at times, and at others by themselves.

From ninety-eight to ninety-nine percent of the time humankind has been around, we were hunters and gatherers. Agriculture is only a relatively recent development, dating back some 16,000 years. Yet it only required 16,000 years to produce the civilization we have today! I find that fact highly unlikely by mere chance. Why didn't we develop civilization 50,000 or 100,000 years ago?

Even when we find time travelers together with aliens, the tall, blonde, blue-eyed, white-robed time travelers from our future establish the fact that they are in charge of this operation. What I find ironic

---

3   J. Oberg, "Terraforming," *Astronomy*, May 1978, p. 9.

about this paradigm is that today we consider these aliens superior in intelligence and technology, whereas in our future they are mere apprentices to the pure human chrononauts. In other words, we eventually progress far beyond the very aliens most people would fear today.

In answer to my questionabout time travelers or aliens: both are correct. These chrononauts exert a great influence on our development, and show a larger interest in our spiritual unfoldment. That is logical, since they are us in the future and have a greater stake in our welfare.

Is it real?

For those of you that think the time traveler regressions my patients experienced are some sort of hoax, let me assure you that none of these patients sought publicity. I approached them for permission to publish their cases in this book.

My own technical competence with hypnotic regression has been established since 1974. *The Search for Grace*[4] was a book detailing the past lives of a patient I called Ivy. Her most recent life as Grace Doze, who was murdered on May 17, 1927, was verified by an independent researcher hired by CBS. This case stands today as one of the most documented cases of reincarnation of this century. It was first aired as a television movie by CBS on May 17, 1994, and has been repeated several other times.

A meeting of the American Psychological Association was held in New York City in 1987. One of their committees concluded that UFO abductees represent a *normal* segment of our population. They come from a wide variety of educational and occupational backgrounds, but their encounters simply could not be explained on the basis of psychopathology. There were also just too many similarities in reported descriptions to suspect fraud.

The scoop-shaped scars found on abductees are real. Flesh has most certainly been removed from these areas of their bodies. Furthermore,

---

4   Goldberg, *The Search for Grace* (Llewellyn, 1997).

the moving through solid objects, such as doors and walls, can be explained through hyperspace and fifth-dimensional paradigms involving parallel universes.

The credibility of my patients reporting their experiences with chrononauts is extremely high. None of them sought attention or media interviews. These people do not benefit in any way from inclusion in this book. I find many common traits in the description, dates, and activities of the chrononauts from people of different countries who do not know each other.

Many of the paradigms I reported are unique, so these individuals couldn't have read about them prior to their hypnotic regressions. I have personally seen their scars. No conventional hypothesis satisfactorily explains what my patients report. It is only the prejudice that society fosters upon us that causes us to reject any theory that appears to go against the "norm."

We can look back to 1954, when a rather large number of UFO sightings were reported, to note just how credible some of these early reports were. The following appeared in the renowned journal *Science,* written by the astronomer Dr. William T. Powers:

> In 1954, over 200 reports over the whole world concerned landings of objects, many with occupants. Of these about 51 percent were observed by more than one person. In fact, in all these sightings at least 624 persons were involved, and only 98 of these people were alone. In 18 multiple witness cases, some witnesses were not aware that anyone else had seen the same thing at the same time and place. In 13 cases, there were more than 10 witnesses.[5]

My work with age progression and future life progression supports the ability to perceive our future and some of the technological advancements reported by my patients. The reports of OBEs also fit in with my experience in conducting regressions and progressions. All of these factors suggest very strongly that these chrononauts' reports are accurate.

---

5   W. T. Powers, "Analysis of UFO Reports." *Science,* 156, April 1967, p. 11.

One message that the time travelers have been trying to impart to us throughout history is that each of us is unique and possesses infinite potential for spiritual as well as technological growth. We are each, as individuals, responsible for this growth. By establishing and maintaining a connection with our Higher Self, we can be more in harmony with a larger whole—infinity.

The natural consequence of this system is a higher level of the development of feelings of love. I am not referring to the codependency form of neediness that passes itself off as "love" by most of society. This form of love develops our capacity to commune with infinity. This allows us to feel good about ourselves and connected to the elements and people around us. The superconscious mind self-hypnosis technique is a simple way to attain this goal.

We must always remember that all areas of life are subject to exact metaphysical laws, which, if known and correctly applied, can bring about apparent miracles—either within the lives of ourselves or others, or even throughout the universe as a whole.

Is there an end to time?

To contemplate an end to time is to consider if change has an end. The Austrian physicist Ludwig Boltzmann long ago visualized the end of the universe (and therefore the end of time) as the attainment of maximum entropy by the universe as a whole. At some undefined date in the future, according to this conjecture, nothing will be hotter or colder than anything else. The slowest radioactive elements will have decayed into stability. The stars will have radiated away their furious energy, warming the frigid dust of interstellar space to a fraction of a fraction of a degree. Earth and its sister planets, their rotation slowed by friction with cosmic dust and gases, will have fallen out of orbit into the Sun. Humanity itself will be long extinct. In this burned-out universe, there will be no change by which time can be observed or measured. In some abstract, metaphysical sense, time may still exist, but, scientifically speaking, it will have ended.

Our universe is currently expanding, but it is estimated that in twenty-five billion years (roughly forty billion years after the big bang), the mutual gravitation of the receding galaxies will slow this expansion to a halt and eventually reverse it.

Forty billion years following this new contracting universe, another big bang will occur, and this cycle will begin all over again. The big bang which began "our" universe was also the bang which ended a previous one; the end of our universe will also be the beginning of another.

The evidence supporting this theory is admittedly tenuous. It includes, among other things, estimates of the rate at which the most distant known galaxies, at the very edge of the observable universe, are receding from the Earth. These measurements, some astronomers believe, indicate that the expansion of the universe is in fact slowing down, but their interpretation is blurred by the fact that at those remote distances the astronomers cannot clearly distinguish the effects of space, time, and motion. Their place in the universe's time scale is also inferred from their distance. We see galaxies at a distance of five billion light-years, not as they are now but as they were five billion years in the past—and if the estimate of distance is off, so is the estimate of time.

Another piece of evidence for this universe-recycling theory comes from the inexplicable abundance of some heavy elements on our planet. Some scientists speculate that this represents debris from a previous universe. There must, according to these scientists, have been at least one previous universe.

But suppose the universe won't be recycled. What are our choices then? Let us review our future astrophysically in detail.

Although the Big Bang created our universe approximately fifteen billion years ago, the laws of physics suggest that our expanding universe will eventually contract. The ultimate result will be an eventual collapse of our universe into a fiery cataclysm known as the Big Crunch, in which all life will simply be vaporized by this excessive heat. The only hope humankind has to escape this eventual destruction is by moving through hyperspace to a parallel universe that is alive and well.

Einstein's general theory of relativity predicted that the fate of the universe is with one of two possibilities:

1. The universe will continue to expand forever until its temperature approaches absolute zero.

2. The universe will contract into a fiery ball in which its temperature approaches infinity. This is called the Big Crunch.

These two options are not attractive. Either our Type III civilization beings freeze in an open universe as illustrated by option 1, or become vaporized in the closed universe of option 2. We don't know which option is likely. The critical factor is if the average density of the universe is greater than 10 to 29 grams per cubic centimeter. If it is, then the Big Crunch will occur. The universe will continue to expand if the average density is less than this figure.

In either option, a Type III civilization will die unless it escapes via hyperspace. Computer calculations by the late Columbia University physicist Gerald Feinberg demonstrated that moments after creation our four-dimensional universe expanded at the expense of the twin six-dimensional universe.

Our six-dimensional universe twin may gradually expand as our own four-dimensional universe collapses. Just moments before our collapse we may be able to enter the now enlarged six-dimensional universe and avoid our previous fate. Of course by that time we will have mastered hyperspace travel and our future should be secure. We can thank the time travelers for our eventual salvation.

Bibliography

Aharonov, Y., D. Alert, and S. D'Amato. "Multiple-Time Properties of Quantum Mechanical Systems." *Physical Review,* 1985, 32 (32).

Allegro, J. M. *Mystery of the Dead Sea Scrolls Revealed.* New York: Gramercy Publishing Co., 1981.

Arnold, Kenneth, and P. Ray. *The Coming of the Saucers.* Amherst, WI: Self-published manuscript, 1952.

Barker, Gray. *They Knew Too Much About Flying Saucers.* New York: University Books, 1956.

Barrow, J. D., and F. J. Tipler. *The Anthropic Cosmological Principle.* Oxford: Oxford University Press, 1986.

Bauval, Robert, and A. Gilbert. *The Orion Mystery.* London: William Heineman, 1994.

Beck, T. R., and J. B. Beck. *Elements of Medical Jurisprudence.* Albany, New York: Little & Co., 1851.

Beckley, T. G. *The UFO Silencers.* New Brunswick, New Jersey: Inner Light, 1990.

Bender, Albert K. *Flying Saucers and the Three Men.* Clarksburg, West Virginia: Saucerian Books, 1962.

Budge, E. A. W. *The Book of the Dead.* London: Longman & Co., 1895.

Burden, B. "MIBs and the Intelligence Community." *Awareness,* Spring 1980.

Clark, Jerome. "Mystery Lights, Fires and Mass Hysteria." *Nexus New Times*, 1995, 2 (25).

_____. *The UFO Encyclopedia*. Detroit: Omnigraphics, Inc., 1996.

Cochrane, A., and K. Callen. *Dolphins and Their Power to Heal*. Santa Monica: Healing Arts Press, 1992.

Condon, Edward U. *Scientific Study of Unidentified Flying Objects*. New York: Bantam Books, 1969.

Cremo, M. A., and R. L. Thompson. *Forbidden Archeology: The Hidden History of the Human Race*. Los Angeles: Bhaktivedanta Book Pub., Inc., 1993.

Davies, P., and J. Brown, eds. *Superstrings: A Theory of Everything?* Cambridge: Cambridge University Press, 1988.

Devney, S. "Beware of the Diabolical Men-In-Black!" *UFO Universe*, Summer, 1989.

DeWitt, Bryce S. "Quantum Mechanics and Reality." *Physics Today*, September 1970, 30–35.

Evans, H. *Mysteries of the Mind, Space & Time*. Westport, Conn.: Orbis, 1992.

Fort, Charles. *The Book of the Damned*. New York: Henry Holt and Company, 1941.

Fuller, J. G. "Flying Saucer Fiasco." *Look*, May 4, 1968, 60.

Gamow, G. *The Birth and Death of Our Sun*. New York: Viking, 1952.

Goldberg, Bruce. *Soul Healing*. St. Paul: Llewellyn Publications, 1996.

_____. *The Search for Grace: The True Story of Murder and Reincarnation*. St. Paul: Llewellyn Publications, 1997.

_____. *Past Lives—Future Lives*. New York: Ballantine Books, 1988.

_____. *Peaceful Transition: The Art of Conscious Dying and the Liberation of the Soul*. St. Paul: Llewellyn Publications, 1997.

_____. *New Age Hypnosis*. St. Paul: Llewellyn Publications, 1998.

_____. "Quantum Physics and Its Application to Past Life Regression and Future Life Progression Hypnotherapy." *Journal of Regression Therapy*, 1973, 7(1), 89–93.

_____. "Depression: a past life cause." *National Guild of Hypnotists Newsletter*, 1993, Oct/Nov, 7, 14.

_____. "The Clinical Use of Hypnotic Regression and Progression in Hypnotherapy." *Psychology—A Journal of Human Behavior*, 1990, 27(1), 43–48.

_____. "Treating Dental Phobias through Past Life Therapy: A Case Report." *Journal of the Maryland State Dental Association,* 1984, 27(3), 137–139.

Group, D. *The Evidence for the Bermuda Triangle.* Wellingborough, England: American Press, 1984.

Hall, A. *Signs of Things to Come.* London: Aldous Books, Ltd., 1975.

Hall, Manly P. *The Secret Teachings of All Ages.* Los Angeles: The Philosophical Research Society, Inc., 1977.

Harrison, M. *Fire From Heaven: A Study of Spontaneous Human Combustion.* New York: Methuen, Inc. 1976.

Hawking, S. W. *A Brief History of Time.* New York: Bantam, 1988.

Hawkins, G. S. *Stonehenge Decoded.* New York: Dell, 1966.

Holzer, Hans. *The Psychic Side of Dreams.* St. Paul: Llewellyn, 1994.

Kaufmann, W. J. *Black Holes and Warped Space-Time.* San Francisco: Freeman, 1979.

Keel, John. *The Mothman Prophecies.* Avondale Estates, Georgia: Illuminet Press, 1991.

_____. *The Complete Guide to Mysterious Beings.* New York: Doubleday & Co., 1994.

Michell, J. *The New View Over Atlantis.* San Francisco: Harper & Row, 1983.

Moody, Raymond. *Life After Life.* New York: Bantam Books, 1975.

Moore, W., and Charles Berlitz. *The Philadelphia Experiment.* New York: Grosset & Dunlap, 1979.

Morris, M. S., and K. S. Thorne. "Wormholes in Spacetime and Their Use for Interstellar Travel: A Tool for Teaching General Relativity." *American Journal of Physics,* 1988, 56, 411.

Morris, M. S., K. S. Thorne, and U. Yortsever. "Wormholes, Time Machines, and the Weak Energy Condition." *Physical Review Letters,* 1988, 61(13), 1446–1449.

Murray, M. *The God of the Witches.* New York: Oxford University Press, 1970.

Neal, R. "Generations of Abductions: A Medical Casebook." *UFO Magazine,* 1988, 3(2), 22.

Oberg, J., "Terraforming." *Astronomy,* May 1978, p. 9.

Penrose, R. *The Emperor's New Mind.* Oxford: Oxford University Press, 1989.

Pike, Albert. *Morals and Dogma of the Ancient and Accepted Scottish Rite of Freemasonry.* Charleston, SC: A.M. 5632, 1950.

Polkinghorne, J. C. *The Quantum World.* Princeton, N.J.: Princeton University Press, 1984.

Powers, W. T. "Analysis of UFO Reports." *Science,* 1967, 156, 1.

Roy, P. *Mahabharata.* Calcutta: Bharata Press, 1978.

Sagan, Carl. *Cosmos.* New York: Random House, 1980.

Sagan, Carl, and I. S. Shklovskii. *Intelligent Life in the Universe.* San Francisco: Holden-Day, Inc., 1966.

Sanderson, Ivan. *Uninvited Visitors: A Biologist Looks at UFOs.* New York: Cowles Educational Corp., 1967.

Saunders, D. R., and R. R. Harkins. *UFOs-Yes!* New York: The World Publishing Co., 1969.

Silk, J. *The Big Bank: The Creation and Evolution of the Universe. 2nd ed.* San Francisco: Freeman, 1988.

Talbot, M. *Mysticism and the New Physics.* New York: Bantam Books, 1980.

Thorne, K. S. *Black Holes and Time Warps: Einstein's Outrageous Legacy.* New York: W. W. Norton & Co., 1994.

Tipler, F. J. "Rotating Cylinders and the Possibility of Global Causality Violation." *Physical Review D.,* 1974, 9, 2203.

Trefil, J. S. *The Moment of Creation.* New York: Macmillan, 1983.

Vaughan, A. *Incredible Coincidence.* New York: J. B. Lippincott, 1979.

Weinberg, S. *The First Three Minutes: A Modern View of the Origin of the Universe.* New York: Basic Books, 1988.

Wheeler, J. A. *In The Mathematical Foundations of Quantum Mechanics,* edited by A. R. Marlow. New York: Academic Press, 1978.

Wilford, John Noble. *The Riddle of the Dinosaur.* London: Faber and Faber, 1986.

Wilkins, Harold. *Mysteries Solved and Unsolved.* London: Odhams, 1958.

Wolf, Fred A. *Parallel Universes.* New York: Simon and Schuster, 1988.

Zee, A. *Fearful Symmetry.* New York: Macmillan, 1986.

Index

☽ LOOK FOR THE CRESCENT MOON

Llewellyn publishes hundreds of books on your favorite subjects! To get these exciting books, including the ones on the following pages, check your local bookstore or order them directly from Llewellyn.

Order by phone

- Call toll-free within the U.S. and Canada, 1-800-THE MOON
- In Minnesota, call (612) 291-1970
- We accept VISA, MasterCard, and American Express

Order by mail

- Send the full price of your order (MN residents add 7% sales tax) in U.S. funds, plus postage & handling to:

  Llewellyn Worldwide
  P.O. Box 64383, Dept. (K307–7)
  St. Paul, MN 55164–0383, U.S.A.

Postage & handling

[For the U.S., Canada, and Mexico)

- $4.00 for orders $15.00 and under
- $5.00 for orders over $15.00
- No charge for orders over $100.00

We ship UPS in the continental United States. We ship standard mail to P.O. boxes. Orders shipped to Alaska, Hawaii, The Virgin Islands, and Puerto Rico are sent first-class mail. Orders shipped to Canada and Mexico are sent surface mail.

International orders: Airmail—add freight equal to price of each book to the total price of order, plus $5.00 for each non-book item (audio tapes, etc.).

Surface mail—Add $1.00 per item.

Allow 4–6 weeks for delivery on all orders.
Postage and handling rates subject to change.

Discounts

We offer a 20% discount to group leaders or agents. You must order a minimum of 5 copies of the same book to get our special quantity price.

Free catalog

Get a free copy of our color catalog, *New Worlds of Mind and Spirit*. Subscribe for just $10.00 in the United States and Canada ($30.00 overseas, airmail). Many bookstores carry *New Worlds*—ask for it!

Soul Healing
Dr. Bruce Goldberg

George: overcame lung cancer and a life of smoking through hypnotic programming.

Mary: tripled her immune system's response to AIDS with the help of age progression.

Now you, too, can learn to raise the vibrational rate of your soul (or subconscious mind) to stimulate your body's own natural healing processes. Explore several natural approaches to healing that include past life regression and future life progression, hypnotherapy, soulmates, angelic healing, near-death experiences, shamanic healing, acupuncture, meditation, yoga, and the new physics.

The miracle of healing comes from within. After reading *Soul Healing,* you will never view your life and the universe in the same way again.

1-56718-317-4, 6 x 9, 304 pp.   **$14.95**

"This is simply the most easy-to-use and complete system of self-hypnosis available without a prescription."

–Dr. Bruce Goldberg

New Age Hypnosis

Dr. Bruce Goldberg

We spend seven hours of every 24-hour day in natural hypnosis. This affords us a tremendous opportunity to grow spiritually, if only we could learn to maximize this state.

Now you can, with the most comprehensive self-hypnosis program available. Under the guidance of a trained and experienced hypnotherapist, you will learn how to place yourself into a hypnotic trance and experience various metaphysical approaches from past life regression to superconscious mind taps, out-of-body experiences and soul plane ascension techniques. You can also learn how to become a New Age hypnotherapist, if you so desire.

Upon completion of this book, you will understand hypnosis, its characteristics and stages. You will be able to induce a hypnotic trance, deepen it, maximize a clinically beneficial state and return to the normal waking state a more spiritually evolved soul.

1-56718-320-4, 6 x 9, 240 pp., illus.   **$12.95**